Text, Talk, Date, Mate

Patsy Isles

Text, Talk, Date, Mate:

online dating success
for women over 50

duafe *books*

Published by Duafe Books, 2018

duafe books

© Patsy Isles 2018

A CIP catalogue record for this book is
available at The British Library

ISBN 978-1-9996732-0-8

Some names have been changed to protect identities

Typeset in Baskerville
Cover design by Karl Weber

Text, Talk, Date, Mate

For
Mary Anna Antoine

Contents

Acknowledgements

There are many people who have helped in the writing of this book. First and foremost, thanks to all the men I had first dates with in my two years online. Thanks to my daughter Malika and partner Gérard. Thanks also to Joy Francis for her inspiration and the exchange of dating stories over dinner at Delice. Thank you Lorna Archer for sister love and a sofa to kip on in the re-location 'early days'. For sharing your experiences and invaluable advice thanks to Halima Mohamed, Ron Griffith, Elizabeth McNicholls, Alison Walcott, Perpetua Egan, Sherif Mehmet, Gloria Inyang, Patrice Ennis and Sherrill Atkins. And not forgetting the Dating SOS ladies I haven't yet mentioned: Philomena Francis, Suzanne Lyn-Cook and Subreena Charlemagne-Odle. To my oldest friends and CDWM sisters: Denise Chance, Dionne Ible, Pauline Jolly-Hunter and Paula Clarke-Little. Eternal thanks for the meals, jokes and wisdom over many wonderful years. And for the world's best coconut sauce and his insightful 'manspective' on life and love thanks to Darrell Alkebulan, my brother from another mother.

Introduction

I spent my twenties and thirties co-habiting, then married, to the same man. While many of my friends were out at the weekends dating, partying and avoiding the prospect of settling down I'd become a wife and mother with no interest in how the dating scene was re-modelling itself. But just a few years into my thirties the gradual decline in my marital bliss reached its inevitable end.

Then after years of self-imposed singledom, another five-year relationship followed. I imagined this was it: that we'd be together until the end. But, in my late forties I found myself single again.

Thrust back into the dating world, I was in for a culture shock. Mortified by the humiliation of previous knock backs, men had given up approaching women. According to them, women were at fault – their idea of playing 'hard to get' having morphed into frostiness at best, open hostility at worse. Now men had decided it was easier not to bother. And with the female pack mentality kicking in on nights out, women weren't approaching men either. A great big dating sinkhole had opened up that was swallowing any chance of male/female interaction into its dark depths. And online dating had by then evolved enough to fill that gap.

The platform's humble beginning stems back to 1959 when Stanford students Jim Harvey and Phil Fialer matched 49 men and 49 women using punch cards and an IBM mainframe computer. Then, in 1965, Harvard maths undergraduates Jeff Tarr and Vaughan Morrill developed the idea further with the launch of 'Operation Match'. Initially an experiment they hoped would lead them to meet attractive women, by the time the company was sold in 1968 it had received a million respondents, each having paid $3 to fill in its relationship questionnaire.

Fast-forward to 1995 and computer dating had morphed into online dating with the launch of InteractiveCorp's Match. com, the first commercial online dating site. It was impossible to predict just how huge the idea would become. Today the industry is flourishing. Worldwide there are 75,000 dating sites and apps with 66% of users having reported success in finding a partner. The sector continues to grow exponentially. Market research group Mintel estimates its future UK worth at £225m by 2019 and according to research by eHarmony, one in two relationships will start online by 2031. There are 91 million dating app users worldwide and in the UK alone more than 5.7million people use dating websites every month. But despite the fact this has become a thriving multi-billion pound industry worldwide, some remain skeptical. I was at first, having heard numerous scare stories of scammers conning women out of their life savings. But in a world where downloading apps has become the way to do everything from language lessons to mindfulness; from takeaways to interior design, mobile dating has become the norm.

This book started life as a blog, a few months after I joined my second dating site. But I needed a context, a theme. Living in a place as multi-culturally diverse as London, it just so happened that the men I dated were from all over the globe. So *The A to Z of Dating: Hunks, Hoods and Hippies from A-ruba to Z-ante* was launched. The idea was to document the dates I had with men from an A to Z of countries. Most of whom I'd met through dating sites, a few through good old-fashioned fate. Over time, however, I also learned lessons from the men I messaged or spoke to but never dated so, in turn, never made it to the blog. I wanted to capture those experiences too and share them in a practical way. The idea for this book was born.

What I discovered was a way to weed out the scammers from the suitors by following each of the four steps outlined in this book. Each step encourages you to get to know your date through a different form of communication.

The problem nowadays is we're in a hurry. And it isn't our fault. As a society we've become impatient. We're looking for instant gratification and have become conditioned to want it all now. Everything about our modern lives encourages haste. There's no need to log on to our laptops to pick up a tweet, a post, an update because we have computers in our handbags. Want a new coat? Buy it online, 24/7. Not sure of the size? Order a few and send back what doesn't fit. We refuse to wait for anything. Including our soulmate.

This impatience has changed our expectations when it comes to meeting potential partners. We're moving faster than we did in the past. Social media has given us a false sense of friendship, of intimacy. We open up to people we've never met about our deepest desires. Then we take this into the physical world, meeting people we barely know. So this book slows the process down. It coaxes you to pace yourself. It's about engaging with the technological world while following the best traditional values.

As I went on more and more dates I began to realise that slowing down the process was a good thing. Rather than rush through – or jump past – a stage, each step was effectively an elimination round. Whether you're texting or talking or meeting in person you discover something new about the person you're talking to. And even though, at first, you're both doing your best to impress, everyone gives off clues about their real selves if you know how to look for them. Dating is just like a job interview. Both you and the employer highlight your best qualities. When we're dating we do the same: reveal our best bits without focusing on all the other stuff. We share the top line, but leave the rest of the paragraph unsaid. Follow the steps in this book and you'll learn to pick up on clues to help you read past the first line of the many suitors online, and among them find that one perfect soulmate.

Text, Talk, Date, Mate ensures you feel confident and in control when you're online, from learning how to sell yourself (without feeling like a narcissist!) to choosing the right profile photos. And you'll learn how to spot a scammer and how to avoid being seduced by them. There are also tons of dating anecdotes, each with a lesson attached. I'll share my three basic principles to online dating, some of the dos and don'ts and lots of practical advice. Dip in and out or read it from cover to cover.

This is a book for women who didn't 'date' the first time round. It's for women who remember the days when you fell into 'going out' with someone then fell out of love decades later. Dipping back into the dating world for the first time in 20 or 30 years can be a daunting prospect. This book will help you read the signs in every situation so you feel empowered and in control. You may have already tried online dating, but haven't taken to it. *Text, Talk, Date, Mate* will guide you back with confidence.

With all this in mind, the one thing you don't want to do is limit yourself. So don't restrict yourself to just dating apps and sites. I wrote this book to help you navigate a world that although increasingly popular still remains a mystery to many. But it doesn't mean you should exclude all the other ways you can meet people. Online dating is just one route to finding love. Talk to people, socialize, let friends play matchmaker. Never miss an opportunity to meet, talk or simply smile at someone.

This isn't a set of rigid rules to follow. We're all far too unique for a one-size-fits-all way of approaching the way we date. But there are three things you should keep in your armoury. Three things that will make the whole process a hell of a lot more effective, and which underpin everything you'll read in this book. I'll talk about each in more depth later, but having gone on roughly 150 dates in two years they're the three principles that helped me navigate the virtual dating world.

Men may be the chasers, but it's you the woman who ultimately chooses. Be empowered by this. Living in a patriarchal society means we've begun to believe the hype. But you are, by your very nature, the one in control. You are beautiful because of your wisdom and life experiences. So celebrate your power, go on a few dates, laugh, enjoy male company and use all the tools in this book to choose the right man for you when the time is right.

Hello world

1

Starting out

Dumped. That's where I found myself. It was unexpected, soul-destroying and about something much larger than the trivial argument that ended our five on-off years together. Without warning, I was single and as the weeks morphed into months I struggled to catch up with the reality. One month in, I hoped the phone would ring, I'd hear his voice and we'd get back to normal. Two months in I expected to bump into him as if somehow engineered by fate. By month three I was reluctantly beginning to call him my ex. I knew I had to move on, but wasn't sure how. So, after a conversation with a friend about how I was feeling, she recommended I go online.

I'd never thought of online dating as a serious way to meet a partner. But then the dating revolution came into full force while I was still knee-deep in long-term relationship woes. I had an ex-husband and had now added an ex-significant-post-divorce boyfriend to my repertoire, both of whom I'd met in the physical world at a time when online dating was still finding its feet. Back then, I saw online dating as a last resort. One of those routes you'd use only if you'd exhausted all other avenues: pubs and bars, work colleagues, evening classes, the supermarket, the gym, art galleries, friends, friends of friends, friends of friends of friends…

Had so much changed? Was finding love in some obscure computing cloud really the best option? Not as far as I was concerned. So, I thanked her for the suggestion and decided to do it the way I'd always done it: by going out and meeting people in the physical world.

So, for the next few months, that's what I did. I got out there. I did my best to meet people. Eligible men. And I did meet a few. But everything had changed since I was last single. Men weren't approaching women. Women weren't approaching men. The way we were relating to each other was broken. Something had happened to old-fashioned real interaction that was having a detrimental effect on the way we connected. There were single men and women everywhere looking for partners, but people seemed reluctant to do anything about it.

I joked with men I chatted to on nights out about my so-called 'anthropological research' into dating habits as I watched how the singletons behaved. Most of the under 25s spent their time posting the night's events to Instagram, Twitter or SnapChat. Clearly more concerned about interacting with their phones than real people, they'd chat for 30 second bursts then spend hours taking hundreds of pictures and video clips to edit their nights out for their timelines – seriously, why talk to one person when you can share with thousands simultaneously? And most of the over 45s had lost the bottle to actually start a conversation with the person standing in arm's reach for fear they'd be ignored. As social beings, the whole world had become inept. No one was living in, or enjoying, the moment.

On my jaunts I also discovered two recurring problems. The first: as a woman in her very late forties my implied classification seemed to have become 'past it'. I'd reached that point where you're no longer noticed by the people you want to attract. It's a time when you reluctantly accept that there are a whole lot of women much younger and fitter than you. And they're getting all the attention – particularly from the not-so-sprightly men. It means most of the people I met were younger than me: considerably, in some cases. The majority of my fellow forty-somethings either married, in long-term relationships or going through divorce.

Of course, I did my best to muster up the courage to interact: to fight my way out of this societal ether. I'd smile when I walked down the street. Make eye contact with everyone, regardless of who they were. It seemed to make sense to just get into the habit of being sociable. With anyone. And it worked. Men smiled back, leading to introductions, conversations, shared jokes and an occasional date. But, inevitably, after the briefest of conversations it was clear that these men were either way too young or way too taken. As wonderful as is it is to meet people in the physcial world – and it really is – the grand, hopeful beginnings led me nowhere time after time after time.

You see, in the physical world we know nothing about the people we're meeting. They are empty containers waiting to be filled. It's exciting, yes, but frustrating, too, when you realise things can go no further. And this leads to the second of the reoccurring problems. Discovering the man you're dating wants children when you're physically, or mentally, past it is a poignant reminder of your own waning fertility.

Added to this, as a black woman I was constantly being reminded through the press or oft-skewed statistics that we were at the bottom of the pile. A group supposedly the least attractive, prone to depression, angry, who reportedly pay more to get into clubs or who are least likely to be contacted online by men. *Any* men. And all this despite the cultural appropriation of our physical-ness on social media, in magazines, by social influencers.

As the months passed, finding someone of a similar age and outlook began to feel impossible. There were few places I could go to meet them and I'd exhausted the spots I'd found. When I next saw the friend who'd suggested online dating I explained how difficult it was to meet people in the physical world. She listened then encouraged me again, 'What do you have to lose?' She said.

She had a point.

Even when I agreed to sign up I did so reluctantly. So reluctantly I told myself I'd just fill in the profile but not subscribe. There was something about having my picture on display to the world that made me feel uncomfortable. Surrounded by friends looking for any opportunity to sell its merits I joined e-Harmony. The first step was a full-on questionnaire and over the next week I filled it in, a little at a time. I added a picture. Just one. A headshot (never a good idea as I came to learn). I clicked a button and my profile went live. By the end of the first day I'd heard nothing. A second day came and went. On day three, I checked my e-Harmony inbox. Someone had sent me a message. Instantly, I felt nervous. I promised myself I'd look at it that evening, but when I got home, I didn't. I swayed between curiosity and disinterest. As a novice, I couldn't even bring myself to visit the site for fear my potential suitor would see I'd been online and wonder why I hadn't responded. I ended the day feeling really anxious about the whole thing. The problem: I simply wasn't ready.

Early adopters

We've all heard of early adopters – those people that jump on any new gadget as soon as it's released. They're on the ball. Ahead of the game. They're the ones that set up tents on the pavement outside the Apple store, queuing overnight just to be the first to get their hands on the latest iPhone. These people know everything about the new gizmo because they've swotted up on it for weeks beforehand. Comfortable with all its functions by the end of day one, they're already experts.

But when it comes to online dating, early adopters are a different breed. If expert is at the North Pole they're at the South. They've signed up prematurely and aren't convinced it will work. They know peanuts about the process, don't trust it and lack the motivation to figure it all out. Maybe a friend has recommended a site to join, or even signed them up as a favour. In short, these early adopters have jumped straight into a pool that's a little too deep. Classic signs are those with incomplete profiles, who vow to fill in the rest soon. They haven't posted a picture for fear of being recognised. The list of qualities they're looking for in a partner is often empty, as are many of their own personal details. They're not committing because of one (or more) of the following:

- They want it to fail so they can tell someone 'I told you so'.
- They don't believe they'll find someone online.
- They're hoping to get back with an ex
- They're not over their divorce/separation/loss of partner
- They secretly believe everyone online is a crazed stalker.

I know all this because I was an early adopter. I didn't realise it at the time, but thinking back it was obvious. Even as I filled out the questionnaire I didn't believe I'd meet someone. Email messages would ping into my inbox and I wouldn't reply to them – even when I thought the person sounded interesting. I just hadn't gotten over this irrational fear I had for people I hadn't met in the physical world. And it was because of all the bad things I'd heard about online dating. I was suspicious of why these men were on dating sites, despite being ignorant of the fact that I was on them too. It's true that receiving complimentary emails helped me realise I *was* still visible – and attractive – to the opposite sex, but I wasn't quite ready to interact just yet.

If you're an early adopter you drag your feet and pretend

you're committed. Sometimes you join up just to stop your friends from hassling you to 'get back out there'. It's not that you don't want to. You do. It's just that the whole thing is so overwhelming.

When you sign up you're suddenly exposed to thousands of potential suitors. Just the thought of that can be daunting – as is getting your head around how to use the site in the first place. Then you're plagued with feelings that the whole process will fail. And if you don't believe it can work, it more than likely won't.

So, how do you know if you're an early adopter? Well, if you're anxious about joining up, that's fine. It's normal to feel nervous when you embark on anything new. If you can persevere, you'll be surprised at how quickly you become comfortable with the site and its functions. But, if what you're feeling about the process is closer to skepticism, the best thing is to do nothing. Don't sign up. Give yourself time. Otherwise, you're being unfair to the thousands of other people on the site who are serious. Just put yourself in their place. Imagine about how it might feel to find the profile of someone you think is the perfect fit only for that person to be an early adopter. Although they don't realise it, early adopters are time wasters. Getting them to commit to the process is impossible because they simply don't believe in it.

But one thing we can all do, and that includes early adopters, is think about what kind of person we're hoping to find.

Who is your dream partner?

At first, I didn't make conscious decisions about the kind of person I wanted to be with. I'd go on dates and we'd either click or face that awkward conversation at the end of the night that put a stop to things there. But we're making subconscious decisions about this all the time. It's that feeling you get when something just doesn't feel right. It could be something as blatant as finding out your date is a smoker when you're not, or something more subtle.

We tune into these emotions, likes and dislikes automatically, but if we're not thinking about them on a conscious level we can end up overlooking the stuff that makes a person a bad fit for us.

Now I was in a position to meet more men, I chose to be more conscious about my choices. So I made a checklist. Checklists work for me professionally, so I thought I'd try the same personally.

I didn't rush it. Over a few days I thought about all the qualities my dream partner would possess. It wasn't exhaustive and the idea was I'd keep it open to change. There were a small number of core non-negotiables, but mostly the list was fluid enough to let some things go and add new qualities.

Your 'dream partner' checklist

On a sheet of paper, make a list of the following headings, adding some of your own. Fill in a list of qualities under each. When you've made your list read it out loud and physically put it out into the world.

✓ Personality Traits: would you prefer someone introverted, extroverted, generous, philanthropic, a thrill-seeker?
✓ Interests: do you want someone with similar or different interests or pastimes to your own?
✓ Physical attributes?
✓ Moral code: how do they live their life? Political leaning?
✓ Non-negotiables – do you want children? Happy to take on step-children? Want a non-smoker?
✓ Cultural background – Do you want someone from the same culture or religion?

Your list should change and grow as you become more comfortable with dating. Allow for some fluidity and accept that you could find someone who fits most, but not all, of your wish list.

Choosing the right app or site

With literally thousands of mobile apps and sites – and more being developed and launched each year – there's an ever-increasing number of ways to help us connect online. There are sites that take a scientific approach; ones that match you based on religion; recommend-a-friend sites; sites for rural singles; sites for those wanting someone in uniform; sites for married people looking for affairs or sites for sugar daddies. There are sites for geek dating, age-gap relationships, Trekkies, LGBTQ, ones for people who love to travel; sites for athletes, people with interesting date ideas and people in prison. There are apps for people who just want sex and, incidentally, ones for people with sexually transmitted diseases. And now, due to the popularity of online dating among more mature people, there are sites specifically to help them find people the same age. There are free sites, subscription-based and dating apps. We're bombarded with TV and radio ads and ads on buses and trains. No matter where we are we're being sold one new site or app after another.

With so much choice, deciding how to get online is a daunting prospect. Most of us go with recommendations from friends – especially if they've been successful finding a partner through it. Should you choose a site where you'll find members who share your interests? Or go for something that matches you on compatibility? What about sites where a friend refers you? To help you navigate the vast number and choose what's best for you it's first useful to look at the pros and cons of the two basic types.

Free sites/apps

Pros	Cons
They're free	More scammers
Large number of users	People looking for hook-ups
User event postings	More 'early adopters'

Subscription-based sites/apps

Pros	Cons
Members are serious	Can be expensive
More focused members	Less choice
More functions	Automatic renewal traps

Pay to Play

What made me choose a subscription-based site when I first signed up? It was the perception that if people pay for the privilege of using a site they had to be more serious about finding a partner. And on the whole, that perception is right. Although, these days, some of the more sophisticated scammers are happy to fork out the money for a subscription if it means they'll get it back ten-fold a few months down the line. But more about them later…

Generally though, people on subscription sites have shown their commitment to the process with hard-earned cash. They've also taken time – and a lot of it – to fill in a relationship questionnaire. They are so comprehensive that any white lies are fizzled out by the law of averages and, on the whole, the people who aren't serious won't have the patience to fill in the questionnaire.

Also, despite subscribing, I didn't join up straightaway. Filling in your profile is free. It's the site's way of drawing you in because as soon as your profile is live you'll start getting emails. Some companies even allow you to reply at least once before you're reminded that, for any further privileges, you'll have to pay. It took quite a few more endearing messages from men on the site to convince me to pay to play. As a fully paid up member I now had access to a greater range of options. These vary but additional features can include: sending/receiving emails; seeing whether your sent emails have been read or deleted; ensuring you appear higher up in searches; gives you access to more user info; see who likes you; use search/advanced search tools.

At anything from £10 to £80 per month, subscriptions can vary. Many of the more expensive offer better rates if you subscribe for longer periods of three, six or 12 months, and once signed up you'll benefit from discounted membership renewals. Always turn off the automatic subscription renewal when you first join to avoid paying again at the end of your subscription when you didn't mean to. You may have to wait a couple of days before you can do this, and most sites make this function difficult to find, so check how it's done *before* you sign up.

Be a 'free' agent

A good starting point for new users, free apps mean no financial commitment – unless you later decide to unlock advanced features.

This means you'll have access to a massive database of users you can browse and contact for free. The free apps are the best way to hone your skills before deciding which to subscribe to.

They also attract users with all kinds of inclinations. Requests I've received over the two years I dated online include married men wanting affairs, a man wanting to be my submissive, another wanting me to be *his* submissive and another looking for someone to accompany him to swingers' nights. Each time, I let them know it wasn't for me but was also quietly impressed by their frankness. Although I'm not into S&M or partner-swapping, there are countless people who are. So as odd or weird or funny as these appeals might seem to some, the people suggesting them understand one important aspect of online dating – to ask for what you want. Whether your request is conventional or unconventional there's someone in the world looking for the same thing. Those things weren't for me, but I applauded their candor, because they each understood the importance of the first of the three key principles that underpin everything you do online.

The three principles

1 Honesty

How honest are you? Maybe you've lied on your cv or called in sick on a workday when you're simply just hungover. We think of these little white lies as harmless, especially if we aren't hurting anyone, but when it comes to dating tiny untruths are amplified when they're discovered. You also give the wrong impression: if you're prepared to lie about your physical appearance or age, for example, how will your date know when you're being honest?

Honesty permeates all aspects of online dating. If you're honest about who you are and what you want, you can begin to focus in on the right kinds of matches. You can also avoid any nasty surprises further down the line.

2 Patience

Waiting is so last century. We rarely wait for anything these days. We can settle arguments with a Google search; buy our groceries at midnight on a Sunday night; or watch a whole season's TV in a day on Netflix. And living in London means I'm already impatient when I'm forced to wait longer than a minute for a tube train. But it wasn't always like this. As a child I remember the time I longed for a pair of penny loafers. They were the 'in' shoe. Almost everyone had them. At school, the girls wore them with their skirts rolled into minis at the waistband and I longed to feel like part of that 'in' crowd. My mum had different ideas though. There was nothing wrong with my current school shoes, so if I wanted a pair I was going to have to save for them. It was the norm. It's what you did when you wanted something but had no means of getting it straightaway. It took me six months to save enough money to buy a pair. I scraped together all my pocket money, did extra chores and gave up eating strawberry bonbons so I wouldn't waste even a penny of the money I earned.

When I finally had enough money to buy the shoes, the penny loafers fad had passed and the girls at school had moved onto the next big thing in shoeware. Waiting had given me a new perspective on my need for them and my desperation had been wrung out in the process.

Sometimes we can get that same sense of desperation when we're dating. We begin to question whether we'll ever meet someone. Whether anyone will even want us. But give in to it and you can either a) settle for a person who really isn't right for you or b) become susceptible to the attentions of a romance scammer.

Patience gives you time to think. Time to reflect on the things that are important (or not). Patience is important not just in the amount of time it takes to meet the perfect person, but also in the way you allow your relationship to develop when you do. Patience gives you the time to see who this new person is. And just like my penny loafers you may find you don't actually want them after all.

3 Flexibility

Remember the perfect partner checklist I mentioned earlier? It's the chance to think about the kind of person you're looking for or what personality traits they should have. It's easy to have polarized views on the things we do and don't want: the black and the white of our 'perfect' partner. But it's the grey area between the two where you'll learn what you're actually prepared to accept in a partner. Stick too rigidly to your checklist and you may never go on a date. Instead, use your checklist as a starting point then let the dates you go on help you refine it.

The one thing we have online is a myriad of choices. New people register every day, meaning the dating pool is ever-expanding. So, allow for flexibility in your list of criteria and you'll meet more people. It will also help you pin down the things that are most important to you in a partner. Think of it as a way to confirm or re-confirm what you do and don't want.

Flexibility also extends to your sense of adventure. Be prepared to try different things. Don't wait for your date to come up with places to meet. Suggest interesting places too. Arrange a date at a wine-tasting evening or chocolate-making class instead of meeting for the usual drink or meal. Keep a sense of flexibility during the dating process and it'll help you refine your checklist, have fun and introduce you to new pursuits.

2

The four big lies

Nowadays, we're swamped with untruths. Whether it's editing out the bad bits of our lives on social media or deciphering what is or isn't fake news, lying has become a post-modern 'truth'. Countless people lie about themselves on dating websites and at some point you'll meet one of them. Until you've exchanged real names, the only information you have about that person is what they've written in their profile and vice versa. There's something about the anonymity of user names that feeds this. And for some, the temptation to lie is too easy to resist.

We all have expectations when it comes to finding a mate and dating sites exploit this. There's never been a time when we can ask for precisely what we want and have some realistic hope of getting it. We can say how tall we want our partner to be, what build or ethnicity. In a virtual world built entirely around us saying what we want, honesty should be easy, right?

Well, yes… and no. It's easy to hide when you're connecting through a mobile phone screen. You can be whoever you want, or pretend at the life you've always dreamed of having, but you have to ask yourself what's the point? Why lie if, at some point, the aim is to meet this person in the flesh?

People will lie about anything and are sometimes far from subtle. However, there are four major areas people most often lie about. And each one stems back to how we feel about ourselves. We hope that by lying in our profile the person we're communicating with will fall for the perfect persona we've created. But even if they do, how do you think they're going to feel when you turn up to the date looking like you've had a full body transplant? Meaningful connections are based on how we connect mentally and spiritually. But they're also based on physical attraction. It's why profile pictures are so important online. It's also the first of the four main things people lie about.

1 Profile pictures

Watch any episode of *Catfish* and you'll see the countless people who have fallen in love with someone they've never met. They've spent months, often years, in email and phone contact. In some cases they've even proposed, all without ever having seen their beloved in the flesh. The people involved had their reasons for lying – maybe they were insecure about the way they looked, seeking revenge or playing a prank – but they all started life with a picture. Most often, a picture of someone else.

Personality isn't the first thing anyone notices about someone. The thing we all do first is see someone. Their physicality. It's visual, something about the way they look perhaps: their smile, the way they carry themselves or that 'can't put into words' aura they give off. We're programmed to react visually because fundamentally this is our default. And it's no different when we meet online because the first thing we'll see, and react to, is a photo.

Of course, falling in love with someone involves getting to know their personality too. But we're living in a world that's visually seductive and because of our technology-induced impatience we're happy to dismiss hundreds of photos – with no thought of 'personality' – with a simple left swipe of our thumb.

Dating apps are designed to play on this obsession we have with images. The first thing you see is a photo. It's why people with more pictures have the best click through rates and why those who don't get few, if any, messages. We don't click through to a profile because we can 'see' a personality. We click through because we like, or are attracted to what we see. And although pictures showing us doing the things we enjoy can reveal aspects of our personality, they too are mainly about attraction – when we're doing the things we enjoy we look happy. A fact backed up by a study carried out by psychologists at Swansea University, which found that simply smiling can make you appear more healthy and attractive.

Of course, there are sites that attempt to go against this grain such as PersonalityMatch (which boasts the tagline: 'Don't fall for the one who catches your eye. Find the one who captures your heart') or LoveFlutter (hailed as the 'thinking person's' Tinder because it analyses your tweets to find a personality match for you), but the most successful are still built on an image-click model. And even the former's tag line 'Online dating without pictures' is followed by smallprint which reads: 'at first' as a reassuring proviso. Developers know that even on niche sites visuals are a key part of the dating paradigm.

Profile pictures are about getting you noticed so make sure you're noticed for the right reasons. If you post a picture of yourself topless and draped across a chaise longue don't be surprised if the kind of attention you get revolves around sex. Which is fine if that's what you want. But don't post semi-naked pictures then expect a man who's interested in your intellect. Ask yourself: how do I want to represent myself online?

Pictures tell stories. Even before the invention of the written word we drew pictures on cave walls. And as children we drew way before we learned to write. There's something innately comforting and easy about browsing through a selection of images. It's like reading, only without the effort needed to form the words into sentences and then interpret them into something meaningful. Our ability to focus is being chipped away at, thanks in the most part to being constantly plugged in to technology. Looking at images takes a lot less brain power.

Pictures also reveal stuff about us, without us even realising. The first thing you have to decide is what you want your photos to say. Are you fun-loving, adventurous, sexy, mysterious, bubbly or thoughtful? Whoever you are, make sure your pictures reflect you.

Never post selfies. Full-length ones taken in mirrors always look a little odd and headshots are often best avoided (see below). Get someone to take a decent photo of you instead. Trawl through all the pictures you and your friends have on Facebook or Instagram. Get a second (and third) opinion. Ask your friends which photos show you in the best light and why. Take your time. The pictures you choose are an important, if not *the* most important, part of your profile so you need to get them right.

<u>*Profile picture dos and don'ts*</u>

DOs

- ✓ **Smile.** Probably the single most important point. You might think you look deep or brooding, but everyone else just sees miserable. If those psychologists at Swansea University say they've found scientific evidence that 'a smile really is the best accessory', why not use your free asset?
- ✓ **Go natural**. No, not in your birthday suit. I mean a natural shot that isn't posed. They're always far more flattering. Posed pictures look a little fake, like you're trying too hard. Even if it isn't, make it look easy.
- ✓ **Include a full body shot** – posting only head and shoulders shots give people the impression you're hiding your body. And, let's face it, no one likes a big reveal on the first date.
- ✓ **Show a variety of pictures**. Choose shots that reflect you on a night out as well as something more casual. You want matches to see you at your best as well as in relaxed settings.

✓ **Show yourself doing what you love.** Get someone to take pictures of you being you. If you have a hobby, a picture of you engaging with that hobby will give your photo real flavour (with one exception – see below). Potential partners will be impressed that you have your own interests. And because we usually smile when we're doing something we like, you'll tick the first point on this list too.

DON'Ts

✗ **Pose topless or semi-nude.** Unless, or course, you're looking for something casual and/or physical.

✗ **Include shots taken at a distance.** Yes, the sunset in the background is breathtaking, but if you're the size of a needle in a landscape the size of a haystack who's going to know what you look like?

✗ **Post a photo with a group of friends.** We don't know you, remember? How will we know which one's you?

✗ **Use photos to set your dating standards.** Post lots of pictures of yourself with only a certain ethnicity or physical build and you could miss out on meeting someone who might not look the same, but is perfect for you.

✗ **Use a cropped photo.** Unless, of course you can completely crop out the remnants of your ex.

✗ **Photo stuff.** This is where someone uploads lots of pictures of themselves looking their best. There'll upload the maximum number of pictures they're allowed. And they'll look fantastic in them all. Except one. In among the haul will be that one photo where they look older, more overweight or with less hair. It's their way of showing you how they look now; their way of hiding in plain sight.

And please pass the next two onto all the men you know: that's your brothers, cousins, sons, friends, work colleagues – in fact any man who's online now or ever. Think of it as a free bit of advice from someone who's seen way too many of the below:

- ✕ **Never post a picture with a carp**. Ok, so you love fishing, but we don't *ever* want to see you hugging a wet fish.
- ✕ **Pose with tigers**. Trust me – it's been done, a lot. We know you're brave and fearless and crave adventure – we get it. We believe you. Now step away from the tiger.

Now, you've picked a selection of photos from the DO list earlier. Which one is best as your main profile photo? If you're looking for a serious partner, never choose the sexiest picture. It'll get a lot of attention, but it might not be the kind of attention you're looking for. Instead choose a picture where you look attractive and approachable. You want to look friendly without too alluring. People wanting casual hook-ups usually look for sexy photos.

Imperfectly perfect

We all have aspects of ourselves we're less than happy with. We can't always conceal these so well in real life but photos give us the power to decide exactly how we want to be portrayed. We're so used to taking photos now that we have hundreds, sometimes thousands on our phones. We can take a picture from every conceivable angle with a myriad of subtle changes of expression or posture. We've become experts at concealing the bits of ourselves we don't like. The sort of stuff we'd prefer to reveal when, and only when, we're ready. But more of this later…

Insecurities leech confidence. And that's the last thing you need when re-entering the dating scene. But there are ways you can disguise the parts of your body you're not so happy with.

What to wear

Can you remember the last time you felt good in your clothes? If you're anything like me, it's not every day and certinaly not always by design. How often have you stumbled on a good look, made a mental note to remember it – then forgotten it a week later? I have too many times to remember.

Good styling comes from knowing your body shape. Look good in your clothes and you'll feel more confident. Feel more confident and it will come through in your profile pictures.

Dress for your body shape

Body shape	Identifying features	Fashion to flatter
Apple	Full chest and back with little or no waist definition	Wear dresses or tops with drapes teamed with skinny jeans or cigar pants
Hourglass	Shoulders and hips are the same width, waist is smaller	Accentuate your figure with bodycon dresses, v-neck dresses and tops

Body shape	Identifying features	Fashion to flatter
Inverted Triangle	Shoulders wider than hips	Wear A-line skirts or bold prints on your bottom half to give the appearance of wider hips
Pear	Hips wider than shoulders	Shrink your lower half with dark colours below the waist and prints on top
Petite	Overall small proportions	Avoid anything fussy including prints. Go for tailored pieces, fitted dresses and block colours
Square	Shoulders, waist and hips	Tone down the androgynous look with peplums to nip in the waist. Choose ruffles and floral lightweight dresses

But confidence (or lack of!) comes from more than just the clothes we wear. Our physicality is also a window to our insecurities. Like the woman who hides her crooked teeth with her hand when she speaks, the man who conceals a birthmark with a lopsided fringe or the woman who wears long sleeves to hide her batwings, many of us worry that some physical aspects of ourselves will make us less attractive.

We all want to appear perfect, but forget there's no such thing. We fail to realise that our imperfections are the very things that make us unique. Instead we look for ways to hide them. Here are just a few of the ways people do this in their pictures:

Head and shoulders only = possibly overweight

Closed mouth shots = problem teeth

Shots taken at a distance = short in height

Heavy make-up = skin conditions

Shots taken in profile = hiding something on your unseen side

None of these should be a problem, but we think they are. Online there's so much choice we worry there'll always be a more perfect option than us. There'll always be people looking for what they perceive as perfect. But no one's perfect. The problem with so-called 'perfection' is the pressure it creates to keep up appearances. If someone's interest in you is that shallow would you even want to pursue a relationship with them?

So, dress to flatter and bolster your confidence. Make your imperfection the most interesting thing about you. Ask potential matches what the least perfect thing is about them. We all have something. Make it a talking point. Online dating is a numbers game. The good thing about numbers is there'll always be someone who's interested in you because you're you.

2 Height

Of the four big lies, this is one men are most guilty of. The reason is simple. We're fed the 'tall, dark, handsome' cliché as soon as we're out of nappies. *Sleeping Beauty*, *Snow White*, *Cinderella*; countless fairy tales end as the handsome (and tall) prince steps in to save the dame and in all the interpretations and re-interpretations, he's never shorter than the lady in distress. And it goes beyond fairy tales and into toys: even Ken has half an inch on Barbie.

Transpose this to the dating world and it's no different.

Women care about height. Most of the single women I spoke to while writing this book admitted they wouldn't say no to a tall man. Men know this, of course, which adds an extra layer of pressure if they're some way off the golden 6ft mark. So what's a small white lie now, if it means they can impress you with their sparkling personality later?

The reality is most men aren't 6ft plus. The average height of a British male is just under 5ft 10in. In the US it's 5ft 9.5in. The height of African men average out at about 5ft 7in and the results worldwide pan out similarly, with only the Netherlands, Bosnia, Denmark and Montenegro boasting average male heights of at least 6ft. That deep pool of eligible men above 6ft that we think exists really doesn't. In real terms, there just aren't enough of them to go around.

Most of the men I dated in my two years online were 5ft 9in or less. They were also the most interesting, witty and attentive. Here's where it's good to be flexible. Don't rule out anyone based merely on height. See how they come across in messages and emails. Judge them on personality, not physicality. A 5ft 9in female close friend of mine was adamant she wanted a man who was at least 6ft. She is now happily engaged to a 5ft 7in man she describes as her soulmate.

3 Weight

We're sensitive about weight us girls. It's not fair that Mother Nature, in all her 'wisdom', begins to pile on the plump from the late thirties – this despite the fact that according to the media we're supposed to maintain waiflike figures to be accepted as 'normal'.

But lying about how you look never ends well.

Believing you look the same as 15 years ago, while entirely possible in some cases, is often a myth. Never use old pictures of yourself if you look significantly different in the here and now, especially if you're carrying more pounds than you did back then. If you do, it's fair to say you're aware of your own deception and are prepared to suffer the consequences. Lying about what you look like is pointless. You'll feel uncomfortable on the date and anxious about having to explain why you look so different in person. But the anxiety you'll feel in the run up to the date is also a good reason to be upfront. You'll fret about how to recreate the 'look' in the photo; what to wear to feel confident; how your date will react when he sees you; whether he'll still like you. And the only thing your date will think when he sees you is: she lied.

4 Age

I met lots of men who lied about their age and most did it to get dates, claiming that fewer women were interested in their profiles as soon as they read they were 55 or above. People hiding their age may well be subtly photo stuffing; with most photos showing them as their younger, fitter selves. But go through all the pictures and there'll be one that's different. In that picture there'll be an older man. How much older can vary… widely. He may be balding. He may have a slight or considerable paunch. He might be slightly out of focus. But there is one thing you can bet on – this is the picture that reflects how he looks now. It's a get out clause if it looks like you'll get to meet each other. He's gently preparing you for what he looks like now. The youthful pictures are to draw

27

you in and start a conversation. Once he's got your attention, he can mesmerise you with his personality. His thinking? You'll be so taken with him as a person that the fact he's much older simply won't matter.

We all want to remember ourselves at our best; reminisce over the good old days when we could attract someone without even trying, but presenting yourself as something you're not with a bunch of dated pictures is still a lie.

3

Writing a killer profile

Of course, I don't mean literally. But it is true to say that when you go online you become a stock item in a gigantic virtual shop. Like any department store there are thousands of products and you have to find a way to stand out from the rest. A great profile ad – the bit where you say something about yourself – can do that and add extra oomph to the outstanding profile pictures you should now have chosen.

We know that online daters respond to pictures first. But if you're serious you'll also want to know more about that person before you contact them. That's where the profile ad comes in and it's surprising how many people either a) don't fill them out at all or b) say nothing about who they are.

Writing a profile ad isn't easy. That's because it's effectively a marketing tool. We're creating the best possible version of ourselves to 'sell' to as many suitors as possible. It's one of the most difficult aspects of setting up a profile because, in reality, when else do we have to write about what makes us so interesting, intriguing, fun, exciting, thoughtful, passionate, kindhearted or generous AND do it with humility or without blowing our own massive trumpet?

Here are two approaches to profile ads:

No picture, no message. I'm sick of time-wasters. Same goes for those idiots that don't fill in their profile ad. Only say hi, and I'll say bye. So, don't waste your time. Oh yes, and don't even bother me if you're allergic to work, or carrying excess baggage.

And

I'd like to meet a fun and genuine man. I love to travel – Cuba and Morocco are next! Interested? But I also love nights in, cuddling on the sofa in front of a good movie. I'm looking for a romantic, who's a good conversationalist and happy to accept my chocolate addiction. Could this be you?

The difference here is in the tone. The first example centres solely on the things the writer doesn't want. It's funny in places, and creative but the only thing we actually learn is that she's negative. It leaves you feeling that she's obviously been hurt in the past and is ready to start any new relationship on the defensive.

The second example couldn't be more different. She's open, playful, gives a real sense of what she's looking for in a partner and then paints a vivid picture of the kind of relationship she's hoping for. Her words feel warm and positive and therefore create a more endearing profile ad than the first.

Words matter. Focus on the negative and that's how you'll come across, even if that's not actually who you are.

I used a third approach and it's the one I'm going to show you how to recreate. Here's my profile as it appeared online:

> *I love trees, writing, the sound of the sea, romantic gestures, summer fruits, laughter, life, the smell of fresh coffee more than its taste, yoga, stimulating conversation, running in the rain, dancing, my daughter's smile, new cultures, new people, photography, playing capoeira, beards on smiley faces (men preferably!), spontaneity, my bare feet on crumbly sand, hugs, full moons, my Kindle, and honesty (even when it hurts).*

Men said they liked it because it sounded genuine and sincere. It was succinct but still managed to say heaps. It avoided talking about what I was looking for (thus leaving that open), and more importantly what I didn't want. Let's face it: it's hard to sell yourself. So here's the secret. The way to let people know who you are is to talk about the things you like, not the things you don't. Nothing defines us better than the things we enjoy. But it also serves another purpose. It's a list of ways to impress you. If you're a G&T kinda gal, what better way for your date to prove he's heard you than to order one for you on your first date? Or maybe he'll grow a beard if you're partial to facial hair – yes, this happened!

How to write a killer profile ad

1. **Write a list of the things you like.** Don't think, just write. Make it a straightforward list of nouns (i.e. chocolate, sunsets, peaches, RayBans, jazz etc). Make it as exhaustive as you like. Come up with practical, interesting and funny things. Enjoy it.

2. **Now write down each of the five senses** – sight, sound, touch, smell, taste. Next to each of them describe something you like that's related to each sense. (i.e. golden sunsets, the sound of children playing, the warmth of the sun on your face, the smell of freshly baked bread, the sweet taste of mangoes)

3. **Mix the words from your first list with the phrases from the second**. You can group similar things together or just keep it all random. You've now got a comprehensive list of the things you like and a profile that reflects your personality.

4. **Avoid using lots of adjectives** or you'll sound like you're full of yourself. Rather than describing yourself as 'chilled' show this with an that captures this (ie I love to meditate in the morning).

So you've chosen the site, your photos and written your profile. Soon the messages will start to fill your inbox and you'll be ready for the first elimination round.

Step One

Text

4

First contact

Christmas was approaching. It was the birthday of a close friend and that perfect time of year. A time when your festive break has started, but you haven't yet reached the Christmas Day anti-climax that's the beginning of the end of the holidays. I was relaxed, the Christmas shopping was done and I had a couple of hours on my hands before I saw a friend. I had nothing to do with myself before hitting the motorway, so I signed up to free dating site, Plenty of Fish.

I'd avoided the free dating sites up to this point – my thinking being that paying customers had to be more serious. But two weeks before the friend of a friend had recommended it. She'd met someone through it and, eight months on, they were 'serious'. Hearing her story I began to think again.

She is a beautiful, successful 40-something woman and she'd found a witty, intelligent 40-something man. Plus, I was edging towards the end of my Match.com subscription and reached the point where the same faces kept appearing in my inbox. The same men sending me winks who never responded when I sent one back.

Besides, if I really was going to practise what I believed I needed to use all the avenues open to me – which included the free sites too. It all made perfect sense.

I signed up…

…and was surprised by what happened next.

Emails began to flood my inbox. The journey to my friend's house took an hour and by the time I arrived I'd received over 60 messages. This was the opposite of the paid sites I'd tried. I'd get a few emails, yes, but nothing like the onslaught I was experiencing now. And it didn't stop there. Over the next few days the messages continued. Free sites have the largest member databases so this made sense. Many of the people I've spoken to about their experiences online have confirmed that they received far more emails when they chose free sites.

Far more interesting though was, for the first time, with a stream of emails to wade through I began to see the different approaches there were to that 'first contact' message. When you see so many all at once, you can't help but compare and contrast. It's like any scientific experiment – the more data you accumulate the more patterns begin to appear.

When I looked through them all in more detail, three types of 'first contact' sender emerged. Three different approaches that can help us all decide how best to communicate. I call them the Chancers, the Cruisers and the Romancers and here's how to recognise them.

1 Chancers

These types are so called because they transmit the same, cleverly-worded message again and again and again. You'll feel as if they're being sincere: that the message has been scribed exclusively for you. Here's a great example I received:

I've just read your profile and loved what I read. We have so much in common and I'd like to get the chance to know you more. What do you say?

It's pleasant enough, right? As a first message it's not too long but better than a simple hi. He's interested and is prepared to say so. That's what I thought too, until I told one of my single friends about it. She didn't respond. Instead, she pulled out her mobile, pulled up the same dating app and showed me exactly the same message she'd received from the same man. His message suddenly lost its appeal. Now he just seemed like a fraud.

Read the message above again and you'll see there's absolutely nothing personal about it at all. Transmitting this message over and over again means he could have any number of things in common with any number of women. This approach is actually quite clever because:

- He's managed to get the word loved in there, which makes him sound like a passionate man.
- He plays on my hopes of finding someone with similar interests, without ever mentioning what those shared interests are.
- There's nothing to show he's *actually* read my profile.

He's made it sound as though it's a message specifically for me, without being specific at all.

He's going for non-specific blanket coverage because the law of averages says if you send out enough messages – that sound as though you've taken a bit of time over them – you're bound to increase your chances of a response.

2 Cruisers

Hi.

That's it. The first message of a Cruiser.

They've seen your profile pic and often haven't even clicked through to your profile. They're just 'cruising', scanning the pictures and sending a simple 'hi' in the hope they'll get a few responses. In a Zoosk survey of 3,000 users the majority of men said this was a good way to get their attention. Maybe that's the reason for this approach: they're seeing it as as a way in. An invitation.

But we all want to feel special and receiving a 'hi' email makes you feel like you're just one of the crowd. Say hi as your first message and it's like you can't be bothered.

I didn't mean to 'chance' it

I was a cruiser once, although I had no idea of it at the time. On one site I pressed the 'send a flirt' button to a man with a smiley set of pics and a laugh-out-loud profile ad. I'd just had lunch and was already late back to work so I thought a 'flirt' would let him know I was interested and take no time. Two for the price of one.

Later, that afternoon my phone beeped a notification. Logging on I saw a message from him in my inbox. There's that moment just before you open a message from someone you like when you feel that buzz of excitement and curiousity. I felt it then.

It didn't last. He'd messaged simply to say how much he disliked people who just said Hi as a first message, before curtly telling me not to contact him again. He obviously wasn't one of those Zooskers. I never used a flirt button again.

3 Romancers

Romancers take their time constructing long, personal introductory messages. They pore over your profile ad to find interesting things to say to you. They take lots of time to craft a personal message – you'll know it's personal too, because there'll be specific references to things you've mentioned. They think about why you might be compatible and tell you. Their messages are interesting, witty, well thought out. They've taken the time to personalise their messages to each person they write to, because they believe in romance.

Remember the message my friend and I received from that Chancer? Here it is again:

I've just read your profile and loved what I read. We have so much in common and I'd like to get the chance to know you more. What do you say?

Here's how a Romancer would approach it:

I've just read your profile and loved what I read. I also like watching the sun setting over water and my daughter's smile. Let's see what else we have in common. What do you say?

It's different, right? Notice how the whole tone has changed? See how, in 35 words, you can achieve a message that's personal and sincere? But it also shows how little time it takes to compose a great first message and make it sound sincere. When someone goes to so much trouble to write to you, take the time to respond – even if it's to say 'thanks, but no thanks'.

So what should you say in the first message?

An inviting first message is about catching someone's attention. It doesn't have to be long, but does need to spark interest and hopefully prompt them to respond.

The easiest way to pen your first message is to:

Read. Their. Profile.

Everything you need to write your message is there. And although men make the first move more often than women on dating sites, if you see someone you like write to them first. Don't let fear of rejection be the thing to stop you. Find something you have in common, something you can laugh about or ask a question about. Keep the message to two or three interesting sentences – it will be personal but won't take too much of your time. If you get no response, don't dwell on it, don't write them again or analyse why you think they're not interested. In other words, don't become attached to the idea of them. Move on.

5

Text revolution

Pick up your phone and count how many methods of communication are available to you that don't involve speaking to a person. Go on, do it now. When I did, I counted 15. Fifteen different ways for me to contact friends and family without actually using my phone as a phone. Admittedly there are a few video call options but on the whole it means writing has largely replaced speaking as the first way we get to know someone. It's interesting when you think about how people used to communicate – through handwritten letters, postcards or telegrams - before the phone call came and replaced all that.

Now, emails, texts, instant messages and social media have shunted phone calls down the grid. It's like we've come full circle. Each age group has its own preferred social media platform. New apps hit the market before we've even grown used to the ones we already have. Some communicate their lives, movements and bodily functions on Facebook. Others prefer the brevity of Twitter or the visuals of Instagram; each format waning and surging in popularity. We're now available 24/7 and finding it increasingly difficult to switch off. Even the anxiety people feel when separated from their mobiles now has it's own official name: *nomophobia*.

It's the norm nowadays to woo someone, having rarely spoken to them. Which means the way we 'talk' to each other is now more about how we 'write' each other, especially in those early days online. It's why this first step involves mastering the written word, but also understanding the way people use words to help you discover more about them. Not everyone finds writing easy, but it's invaluable for picking up hints about a person. Often, written messages will say much more than just the words they contain.

However, there are a couple of things that have evolved as a result of this preoccupation we have with the written word. Both can be experienced during this text phase, when you're simply writing to each other, and both can be problematic.

1 Premature attachment

If you have spent much of your adult life in long-term relationships, you can easily find yourself drawn into this. I spent the first 16 years of my adult life in one committed relationship, so when I was first dating it influenced the way I viewed the men I met. When I started communicating with someone, my first thought was always whether they could be my next long-term prospect. I couldn't help it. My experience of being with a man was linked to long-term commitment. So, before I could relax and enjoy dating I had to shake myself out of this mindset. I had to get to the point where I could enjoy meeting men and going on dates without the weight of commitment forever lurking in the background.

Dating is about being and feeling free. It's about learning who and what you want for your next relationship. You learn as much about yourself as you do the many people you should definitely get out and meet. What it shouldn't be about is hooking up with your first potential match. When you're used to long-term relationships, as soon as you start to feel connected to someone the temptation is to jump in prematurely. You make excuses not to go on dates with other people; stop responding to new messages in your inbox; stop telling your friends because you can sense their disapproval; hide or delete your profile, and all because you're throwing your hopes into this one person.

It's easy to feel like you know someone you've never met. Early attachment happens when you become too close to someone too soon. You've written each other countless messages through the app or site on which you met. You may have even given each other pet names and are sending countless messages to each other, which means they're on your mind most of the day. They're adept at tapping out emotive texts full of all the things you'd love a new partner to say. They send you beautifully worded messages first thing in the morning, a special good night text just before bedtime.

It makes you feel warm inside. Like you could easily fall in love with this person. And all of this before you've even met. Often arranging the first date isn't straightforward. They may be working out of town; contact you to pull out with a last minute emergency and a reason to postpone; or simply too busy to find the time. But all the while they continue to keep you hanging with their heart-warming messages. So you make excuses for them and wait patiently for that first date. This is early attachment. And it can be dangerous because it's what scammers rely on to groom you.

The thing about early attachment is you don't know how you're going to feel if/when you do meet the person. They may have put off your first date for legitimate reasons. Some look nothing like their picture and want you to fall in love with the idea of them in the hope that when you actually meet you won't care what they look like. Then there are the people who never intend to meet you. These serial texters are already in relationships and are unhappy or unfulfilled and want something to fill their time while away on business trips. They're happy to flirt, but not quite prepared to go the whole hog and have an affair. But you'll be on the receiving end and it'll go nowhere.

Either way, if you've experienced any of the above or feel yourself pining for someone before the two of you have even hinted at a meeting you've become prematurely attached.

What to do

- **Don't cut yourself off.** Reply to messages from other people so your focus isn't on that person alone. Psychologically, you'll have less room in your head to develop an attachment.

• **Avoid over-messaging.** If you send a morning message, end it by saying you'll be at work all day and unable to respond to messages to limit the amount of communication you receive/send throughout the day, but don't then make up for it by texting and emailing all evening!

• **Don't become too familiar before you meet each other** in person. So don't give each other pet names and no sharing every little aspect of your day.

• **Don't be drawn in by the 'opposites' effect.** It's easy to fall for someone who's the polar opposite of your ex, especially if the pain of your break-up is still raw. But going from one extreme to the other will just introduce a new set of problems.

• **Let them show not tell.** Don't allow yourself to get too excited by what they've *told* you in their profile. You want tthem to *show* you through their actions as you get to know them.

• **Think of everyone you meet as a one-date wonder.** Always assume you'll have one date and no more.

2 False intimacy

Some people will quickly turn your texting into sexting. But the problem with sexting before you meet is it creates a false sense of intimacy. You'll also potentially compromise your personal security. It's shockingly easy for a scammer to glean personal information about you and then use it to make you feel as if he understands you when, in reality, he's still a stranger.

There's also no way of knowing if you'll be attracted to them in person. Imagine rocking up and André is not quite the hunk he was in the profile photo you now realise is over 10 years old? So, save the sexting until after you've met, have decided you like them and want to get physical.

Taking things to a sexual level before you meet can be dangerous, especially if that includes sending intimate pictures of yourself. You'll have no control over what they do with them, which means intimate pictures of you could end up posted somewhere in cyberspace where you'd really prefer they weren't.

What to do

- **Be direct.** Tell them you're uncomfortable with it and don't allow youself to be pressured. Being direct in this way is empowering because it puts you in control.

- **Don't agree just to avoid being rejected.** There are thousands of people online with new people signing up every day. There really are plenty of fish… You *will* meet someone else, and another and another if necessary.

- **What if I'm not attracted to them in person?** Drag yourself back down to earth by asking yourself this. If you're going to get intimate virtually, make sure you meet first.

- **Remember, this person is a stranger.** Would you start a sexually-charged conversation with a random person sitting next to you on the bus or train? No. They're a stranger. So is the person you've just met online. You may feel close to them, but what do you really know about them?

- **Block them.** If they're persistent or you feel worried or threatened, first tell them you're not comfortable then stop any further contact with them by blocking them.

Sexters are direct. Which means you'll know where you stand. They know what they want and are simply looking for someone who wants the same.

And it's the word choices people make when they're first in contact with you that can help you form your first impressions. So, what exactly do the words we use say about us?

6

What am I saying really?

Before you hit send after writing a message, take a moment to read it. Ask yourself how you'd feel if you were on the receiving end. How would the person reading it perceive you? Quite often we don't think about what we write, what it says about us and the effect it will have.

But thinking about words takes time – and time has become a rare commodity. It's much simpler to tap out a message and send it out into the Twitterspehere, than it is to think about the many different ways our words can be misconstrued. How many times have you received a text message that has left you questioning the tone of the sender? Are they annoyed, upset, being ironic, having a laugh? Our ability to understand the emotions behind the messages we receive hasn't kept up with the speed of textual development over the last few years.

Predictive text has helped move all but a few beyond annoying textspeak (even if we've all suffered from epic predictive text fails as a result!). The internet has expanded our reach – to knowledge, to community and to every part of the globe. We communicate with words more now than we ever have and use an ever-increasing number of social media platforms. In fact, because we're talking less, we've lost the clues we used to pick up on to tell us how someone was feeling. Over the phone, we'd listen to a person's intonation; to whether their voice sounded excited, bored, disinterested, ecstatic. In person, we'd pick up on clues to how they were feeling thanks to their body language, and how their physical presence helped to convey their emotions. Communicating using written words alone allows for none of these things. Often we're using fewer words and shorter sentences, which leads to misinterpretation. How often have you received a text from someone that has rubbed you up the wrong way? Even the way we write can hint (sometimes wrongly) at personality. Use short sentences and you'll sound clipped or angry. Long, flowery ones and you may not get your message across. So, how has the technological world responded? This is how:

And we're using emojis to fill our messages with the emotion that texts and emails strip out. We use them so our words aren't misunderstood. They act as a failsafe to confirm how we're feeling at the exact moment we tap out our message. That is, if we understand the subtle nuances between some of the 2,823 emojis that now exist on various platforms.

Emoji's have made us lazy writers. And they're dominating how we communicate. In 2015, for the first time ever, Oxford Dictionaries Word of the Year, 2015 was this:

It was chosen because it was 'the word that best reflected the ethos, mood and preoccupations of 2015'. So these little symbols are the modern way to clarify what we're saying, to communicate how we're feeling, to fill in the gaps we're now missing in a world gone text message mad.

They also mean we've moved on from the problem of misinterpretation of our words to the misinterpretation of the little pictures we choose. Receive a message containing one of the newer, or less familiar, emojis and you'll find yourself trying to figure out what he could possibly have meant when he added the upside down smiley face (it's sarcasm apparently).

The misinterpretation occurs because no one seems exactly sure of what the more subtle emojis mean. Add to this the fact that the same emoji can appear differently depending on the platform you're using (iPhone, Android, Twitter, Facebook, Mozilla etc) and there is massive room for confusion when it comes to translating them into real words/emotions. So, don't overcomplicate your messages with the more subtle versions of these icons, but equally don't spend ages fretting over what the smiling/crying face at the end of someone's message might mean. If you don't know, just take the emoji out of the equation. Let it go. Breathe. Don't get hung up over the small stuff.

Focus on words not pictures

When you write to someone, imagine what you'd say if they were standing in front of you. That's what you want to capture in your message. When you write what you'd say, you sound like you and it will naturally bring personality to your message. We're programmed to communicate differently when we write. We tend to sound more formal, less human. We also think we'll sound more intelligent if we throw in the kind of words we'd never use when we're chatting to friends. But that won't capture your voice. It won't give a person an idea of how you sound.

Some people worry that their level of grammar means they'll come across badly. And it's true for a lot of people. A Zoosk poll, found that 65% of women and 60% of men said that bad grammar was a 'dating deal breaker'. People with bad grammar were seen as careless, lazy or simply not bothered enough to make the effort. 72% said the same about dodgy spelling.

Writing more like you speak can help you get around this because your personality shines through. An ex-boyfriend of mine was a spelling disaster zone, which he admitted from before the start of our relationship, but I loved it when his messages pinged into my inbox because reading them was like listening to him speak. I could literally hear his voice, and his humour shone through. So capturing your speaking voice can be a way around the whole worry about how 'intellectual' you'll come across.

However if you aren't so confident about spelling or grammar and worried about how you'll come across in your messages, you can at least do the basics. And like most things in our lives these days there's *always* an app that can help :

• **Spellcheck your message**. You can get free spellchecker apps for both iOS and Android phones.

• **Get a free grammar checker** There are, again, countless apps (Grammarly is a particularly good one).

• **Watch out for the most common mistakes below (they're also the ones people find the most irritating).** People get these wrong all the time, so check here first:

Common Mistakes	
Problem	Solution
Using its and it's in the wrong contexts	Say the sentence out loud replacing its/it's for it is to see which one works. It's is a contraction of 'it is'. Its is about ownership. ✓ 'It is a great profile' = It's ✗ 'The pub has it is own beer garden.' = its
Confusing the use of there, they're and their	There for places. Their for ownership. They're is a contraction of 'They are'

Confusing the use of we're and were	Read the sentence replacing were/we're for 'we are' to see which one works. ✓ Do you know where we are going? = we're ✗ Where we are you? = were
Writing 'a lot' as one word (ie alot)	A lot is a large number. Allot means to share something out. Alot isn't a word
Confusing the use of two, too and to	Two refers to the number 2. You can have 'too' much or 'too' little of something. To has a number of meanings including 'until' or 'toward' (ie I'm going to go home).
Knowing when to use your or you're	Say the sentence out loud replacing you're/your for 'you are' to see which one works ✓ 'You are welcome.' = you're ✗ 'You are name is Sam' = your

7

Romance scammers

His first message was pleasant enough and it was clear from his profile that Ezra had led an interesting life. He was American and although he had lived in the UK some years before, he'd gone back to the States when his marriage failed. He was an IT consultant and explained that he was in the UK while he decided if he should settle here permanently. His pictures were all fairly consistent, which made me think that if we got to meet there was a strong chance he'd actually look like them.

His first message was a little formal, but not so much that

he came across as reserved. In fact, it was a comfortable balance between wit and intelligence – certainly enough to prompt me to respond. He wanted to exchange numbers and move off the site almost immediately, but I said I'd like to continue until I knew more about him. So, we exchanged messages all that day. We had similar interests – in the books we'd read, places we'd visited. He was at a crossroads in life, he said, and was trying to decide what he wanted to do going forward. He'd worked solidly for many years and now wanted to sit back and enjoy life. He'd had a successful career back in the States and financially was comfortable enough not to worry about work for while.

I asked him about his last relationship. He explained that he'd been with his last girlfriend for eight years. She was Canadian and he'd eventually moved to Canada to be with her. The relationship had broken down a year ago and feeling that spirit of wanderlust returning he'd decided not to return to the States, but come to England, where he'd worked for a while, to think about what he wanted to do next. I was enjoying our messaging so when he asked again to exchange phone numbers I agreed.

I was feeling hopeful. It's that feeling you get when, after countless IMs, site emails or texts you finally connect with someone. Online dating can be exhausting sometimes. It's like climbing a steep mountain, only getting so far each time before you find yourself hurtling back down. This felt like it could be different.

First thing the next morning, my phone beeped. It was Ezra. A good morning message framed by teddy bears, cerise hearts and balloons. It wasn't my kind of thing, to be fair – yes, teddy bears are cute when you're five, much less so when you're approaching

50 – but the fact I was one of his first thoughts was warming.

Over the next few days we exchanged more messages. Each morning and evening I'd receive a similar fluffy hearts and flowers message. He was complimentary, maybe even overly so, commenting on how beautiful I looked in my profile picture or how warm I sounded on the phone. Our conversations covered deeper and more personal ground as we began to reveal our innermost feelings to one another. When we spoke on the phone, I found myself feeling drawn to his gravelly American drawl. I asked him about his unusual name and he explained he'd been named after his grandfather. We had overlong phone conversations, shared a similar sense of humour and had even discussed when we were going to meet. But by the end of the first week something he said while we chatted made my journalistic hackles rise. He talked about a business deal that was going wrong. It was something to do with the financing of it. He needed to raise £5,000.

He didn't ask me for any money and I didn't dwell on it or ask him any further questions about it. A few days before I'd asked him his full name. So, as soon as I was off the phone I googled the name he'd given me. I found details of his registered companies in the States and in Canada. I also found other pictures of him confirming that he was, in fact the same person. But what I discovered next was the most interesting: he was wanted for fraud.

Internet dating fraudsters – staying safe

Ezra had used his own name and photo, so I don't believe he was an actual scammer. But it was a wake up call because it proved how easy it was to feel drawn in in a very short space of time.

The vast majority of people using dating sites are just like me or you. They're online to date, find a partner, wife or husband. Most of the people you meet will have this intention, even if you eventually find there's no spark. But the anonymity of the Internet is also its downfall. We've become so used to sharing the details of our lives through our computers, we forget that this information becomes a permanent record for those wanting to exploit it. These are the romance scammers.

Get Safe Online says UK 'romance fraud' cost its victims £41million in 2017, with 3,557 reported cases. 55% of all cases are from 40-55-year-olds, 63% are women and it's believed the figure could be considerably higher due to the embarrassment some victims feel, which prevents them from reporting a crime.

So before you share any personal details there's a few things you can do to keep yourself safe. The first acts as a filter for those you may not want to stay in contact with. Use an old mobile phone or buy a cheap one. Then get a pay as you go SIM card to use as your dating contact number. This keeps your actual phone number free of any numbers you may not want to keep and, crucially, means your real number is never in someone's phone you're no longer in contact with. Never give out a landline number. Also, be aware that if someone knows your full name and the area you live they can track down your home address.

How to spot a fraudster

Text messaging or IMs are the first opportunity a fraudster has to draw you in. The best thing here is to follow your gut. If something feels dodgy, it probably is. Some things might not feel that out of the ordinary, others are massive red flags. It's why you should think first before giving out any information or access to your social media profiles. Here are some things to consider:

- **What do you really know about them?** They'll ask lots of questions about you but will avoid answering basic questions such as where they live or work.
- **They're reluctant to use the dating site** to contact you and will suggest communicating off site almost immediately.
- **They'll give you a pet name.** Yes, you'll feel more connected to them, but that's all part of the grooming process.
- **They will either talk about or ask you for money.** It might be for help with a business deal, or to help his terminally ill mother receive palliative care, or to help him get home from an island in the middle of the pacific ocean (yes, really!).
- **They'll ask if they can connect with you on social media.** Our posts reveal so much more about ourselves and our lives than we realise and are a goldmine for scammers.
- **They may look like they've walked off the pages of a fashion magazine.** We all want to believe we can 'pull' someone drop dead gorge. But scammers rely on this.
- **They might encourage you to send intimate photos of yourself.** In some cases, intimate photos have been used for blackmail by threatening to post them online. Never agree before you've met someone.
- **They might send you weird links.** Never click on them. These are often used to get hold of your personal information.

There could also be clues in the way he writes to you. Recent studies have found interesting common ground in the language often used by fraudsters. They found that they seemed to dislike the use of capital letters and used 'ur' rather than 'your'. If the word happened was misspelled as 'happend', the user was 22 times more likely to be a fraudster than if the word was spelled correctly. And if someone is claiming to be from an English-speaking country and their spelling and grammar is atrocious this could also be a sign.

How to be safe online

We're so used to communicating online we forget how exposed our favourite apps make us. Phone GPS systems track and log our movements, social media apps suggest friends, and e-commerce sites use targeted advertising to get us to buy their newest gadget. Think about it. Combine all these things and, with the right access, someone can build a real picture of your life and habits.

We've all heard about the scammers who create tragic, desperate or heart-breaking stories to get people to part with their money. What's more shocking is many of the victims had never met the fraudster in person. It's because we're genuinely hoping to find love and we assume everyone else is too. It makes us vulnerable. And although vulnerability is so often a strength, as far as scammers are concerned it is also our weakness. Vulnerability has become a very lucrative business. If we weren't so susceptible to the idea of true love we wouldn't be so easily scammed. We're pulled in by early attraction and convinced by fake photos, words and sob stories. We are groomed – often over months. And no one is immune – it has happened to women from all backgrounds, educational ability and social status.

However, even with the shocking statistics above, scammers still make up a relatively small number of the people using dating sites. The key is in knowing, first: how to recognise them and second: how to deal with them.

10 Golden rules to avoid being scammed

• **Always use an online handle** to avoid giving away personal information. So Amy_Hackney or Katy@Wellingborough are out, PurpleHaze or GreenMan2 are in.

• **Do a Google Reverse Image search.** It's where you use an image as your search item then Google trawls the net to find websites where the picture appears. It's an easy way to check whether someone has used genuine images of themselves or simply lifted another person's image.

• **Ask to speak via video.** Scammers don't want to be identified. Get them to agree to a Skype, FaceTime or Zoom call asap. If they're reluctant and full of excuses, then there's a reason. And it's won't be a good one.

• **Keep your personal email address secure.** Use the app messaging/mail services when you first make contact and until you've seen the person via What's App video or Skype.

• **Set up a separate email account** for people you meet online. It will keep your personal inbox free of excess emails.

• **Use a pay as you go SIM** in an old mobile so your actual telephone number doesn't end up in the phones of people you'd rather not keep in touch with.

• **Avoid connecting on social media.** Access to your social media accounts can give scammers everything they need to get inside your head. LinkedIn will give them employment background, Facebook will reveal the kinds of friends you have and the places you go, Instagram will show your interests and pasttimes and SnapChat will give them live access to your everyday timeline snaps. Connect with them just through the dating site for as long as you need to feel comfortable.

• **NEVER part with money,** no matter what heartbreak story you're told. They could ask after six days, six weeks or six months, but the answer should always be the same: no. Popular stories to get you to part with cash are: sick children or parents, problems accessing their own money, helping them get home from a business trip or funding life-saving surgery for a family member abroad. However they package it say NO.

• **Always tell a friend you're communicating with someone new.** If your internal voice of reason has been compromised, theirs won't be and they'll keep you grounded.

• **Trust your gut.** Remember, scammers spend a lot of time learning how to seduce people so they're prepared to play the 'long game'. They'll invest time – and lots of it – getting you to fall in love with them before they approach the real reason they're in contact with you. They know what to say and how to act to make you feel like the most important person in their life. They'll tell you they're thinking about you at different points during the day, send you cute messages. They may even send you romantic gifts or talk about the expensive things they own to build a false picture of their lifestyle. If you suspect someone's too good to be true they probably are.

Who's in control?

Dating apps and sites have re-energised men's power to pursue. Online, men send far more emails than women. AreYouInterested. com, found that straight men have to send on average 25 messages to be sure of a response, compared with an average of just 5 for women. Big difference. Men can also approach whomever they like, without the fear of public humiliation if they're turned down. They don't have to face the taunts from their mates if the woman on the other side of the bar turns them down. A reason many men are so reluctant to approach women in the real world.

It's also empowered us as 50+ women. We've taken control of the dating process in a different way. It's given us a way to meet partners that isn't as restrictive as in the physical world. We can more easily find partners of a similar age, wavelength or cultural background. Women receive more messages than men online, which means we can also actively choose. Choose which men to respond to and which ones to ignore. The anonymity of online dating has also given women real power.

I started chatting to Tom one night on a free site. He was a yoga teacher, which I naively thought might elevate him in some 'he's a spiritual being' sort of way. His profile ad gave a sense of his passion for his work and the natural world. His opening message was witty, personalised (he talked about our shared interests) and was neither too short nor too long. We'd exchanged just a few messages – mine fairly lengthy, his responses kept to one or two sentences – when we got onto the subject of cooking. He asked what my signature dish was. I told him then asked him the same. Tom tapped out a response: *I'm not that great a cook, I'm much better in bed.*

It was such a random, unexpected change of topic from 'he of the spiritual realm', that I actually sat upright on my sofa.

The conversation continued:

Tom: Who else are you talking to [online] tonight.

Me: No one else tonight actually. What about you?

Tom: Just you

Tom: [his telephone number]

Me: So should I assume you want me to call that number?

[5 min gap during which there is no response]

Me: It's been really nice chatting to you Tom, but I think we're looking for different things. Good luck in your search.

Tom: Really?

Tom obviously didn't think there was anything wrong with this exchange. He knew what he wanted and was keeping the conversation to the point. The thing is men and women communicate differently. And it's no different online.

Men are, on the whole, creatures of brevity. They're direct. They like communication to get straight to the point. And the quicker the better. What Tom was doing was steering the conversation away from the small talk. He was moving things along so he could get to the point. His point. I on the other hand wanted to know a bit more about him. For me, this first conversation wasn't about how quickly we were going to get into bed, but about discovery, about feeling connected. And there's the difference.

These are, of course, generalisations. But various studies have backed this up. Linguistics professor Deborah Tannen, believes the reason men and women communicate differently is because our focus is different. She believes that: 'men want to report' while 'women want a rapport', meaning that on a basic level, men communicate to pass on direct information, but women communicate to develop a connection. Which does seem to explain what was going on in my exchange with Tom that night.

He was saying: *"I want to 'hook up' with you."*

I was saying: *"I want to find out more about you."*

Sometimes it's good to remember this.

Let's talk about sex(ual) innuendo

I don't even remember why I was up so late. A work deadline maybe, or one of those fall-asleep-in-front-of-the-telly evenings that just creep up on you. I logged in to check some emails and almost instantly an IM flashed up. It wasn't someone I recognised so I checked out his profile. He was younger than me and worked in banking. He had a friendly, smiley face and his profile name (Jimbo) seemed safe and like a man who didn't take himself too seriously. If I'm honest, I wasn't attracted to him. I don't know what all the elements are that make up instant attraction, but whatever they are they weren't looking out at me from his picture. He'd been browsing too, had found my profile and (crucially, I think) saw that I was online right at that moment.

This is how my IM conversation with Jimbo went.

Hello Gorgeous! He typed. It wasn't the most original start.

Hey I typed back. We chatted a little and it was soon clear that dear Jimbo had a great sense of humour. He'd just got in from an after work pub stop with some friends and was still drunk. After a few introductory messages he soon turned the conversation into a quick-fire question and answer session.

Jimbo: *White wine or red?*

Me: *Cinema or theatre?*

Jimbo*: Beach or adventure holiday?*

Me*: Taxi or tube?*

Jimbo*: French knicker or thong?*

Me (out loud): '*What the hell!*'

Quite often when you're online late at night your judgement is impaired. Even if you're not drunk after a night out drinking with your mates, you're mentally and physically tired. And who knows what state the people you're talking to are in. I've received late night messages from men who, when I've responded the next morning, I've never heard from them again. Sometimes what seems a good idea on the back of a few beers and a curry, is the furthest thing from your mind when you wake up to see a message in your inbox from someone you're so not in to. My advice? Put your phone down, rest your head (and thumb) and leave the scrolling to the morning. Online, we can be whoever we want and say whatever we want. It gives people the courage to do, say or write the types of things they ordinarily wouldn't. I'm guessing it's what gave Jimbo the confidence to steer the conversation off piste.

It's the false bravado that comes with knowing if you're rejected, no one will know.

We never contacted each other again. It was just one of those conversations on one of those nights.

When to move on to a phone call

So how long should you wait before exchanging numbers? The answer is going to depend on how you connect with the person you're communicating with. But, avoid texting someone for weeks and months before meeting them (remember that thing about attachment?), or exchanging messages for just a day or two. The point of going through each of the stages in this book is to give yourself time to find out about your match. And you'll discover more about them the more time you give yourself. As a rule, one or two weeks seems sensible for text based communication, depending on the frequency of your messaging. I have messaged for as long three weeks, but that was with a man whom I didn't hear from that frequently.

You want to avoid prolonging this stage for too long because you could find yourself becoming attached to the 'idea' of the person rather than the reality. Get to know them through their words, but move things to a phone conversation so you get a different perspective.

Step Two

Talk

8

Does my voice sound good in this?

One of the things I love at this age is having the courage to say what I actually feel. It's taken me until now to realise that you can say anything to anyone so long as it's said with compassion. But my first phone conversation with Ben, who was 10 years my junior and worked in banking did make me question this briefly.

He'd spent a year travelling, learning something new in each place he visited: salsa in Cuba; skiing in France; yoga in India...

I remember thinking what an inspired idea. We'd connected well through our text messages, had a similar sense of humour and although he wasn't physically the kind of man I was attracted to, I liked how he sounded in his messages. After we'd said hi, and how great it was to finally speak, I asked him about his travel experiences. He was only too happy to talk. About himself. I mean non-stop. Like he needed to get every small detail about his experiences out of his system. His words floated in the space between his phone and mine. I barely had the time to absorb them before he filled the air with more. That one question lasted the entire conversation. Ben was obviously excited by everything he'd done. But wasn't the least bit concened with what might interest me.

I'd exchanged text messages with other men before Ben. I'd had countless email exchanges that I thought had gone well, then fizzled out. I used to wonder if I'd said something off-putting, or if they'd sensed a tone in my voice they didn't like. I soon learned it wasn't worth speculating about. After a time I realised that most times I had no idea why app chats or emails stuttered to a halt. And talking to a 'match' for the first time isn't like a job interview – you're not exactly going to go back to them and ask for feedback on why you've been kicked to the kerb.

When you're about to talk to somone you like, you want it to go well. And after that first conversation you want to like them more. But it also felt a little back to front. Meeting someone in a bar or supermarket means you speak as soon as you meet. Doing it this way took a little getting used to. I'm good at words on the page, at constructing what I want to say with a pen or keyboard. I can control my thoughts and shape how I share them. It's why

I enjoy the banter of texts or instant messages. But speaking to someone you haven't met in person is subtly different. You know there's something you like about them or you wouldn't have got this far. And even if you feel as if you'll connect when you speak it can quickly evaporate when you first hear them. You're also doing your best to find the balance between what you reveal about yourself and what you don't.

Having that first conversation is moving you closer to actually meeting the perfect partner. You've moved on in the process, you're tuning into their voice, their turn of phrase, their humour. You're starting to decide whether there's any chemistry between you. But this is also another point at which your match can be eliminated. People reveal a little more about themselves with each new form of communication they use. Skip this stage and you're missing out on a whole set of clues about who that person is and how you might get on. Our words often say so much more than we intend, so it's important that we think about the language we, and our potential dates, are using. Listen carefully to the things people say. It's the catalyst that, all going well, will lead to more conversations and eventually a date. You're both deciding whether you like each other's tone of voice, way of thinking, humour. You're getting a sense of their character. They're getting a sense of your quirks. You're tuning into the things you can't quite put across in words on a profile ad. It's a necessary step along the road to a date.

If you've managed to avoid them up to now, it's the first time you will truly have expectations (more of this later). You'll be curious about how their voice sounds and may have already imagined it. But nothing can prepare you for how it will actually sound. Voice is important to us. It's because certain tones and sounds have different effects on us.

Another first conversation with a date early on in my dating experience is a good example. His profile picture revealed a tall, well built bald man. His voice, however, was quite the opposite – like a young David Beckham. I've come to learn that the best way to tackle that first conversation is to just do it. Don't try to imagine how he'll sound. Just pick up the phone.

How do I sound?

You can learn a lot about a person from their voice. It's why you should never agree to a date before you've heard them speak. We use all five of our senses to select a mate and the sense of sound comes into it's own during that first phone conversation. Confident and self-assured or shy and prone to one word responses, it's a good idea to pay attention to what you can hear. More than once, I've spoken to someone who comes across very differently over the phone when compared with his texts.

Hearing someone's voice is part of what draws us to someone and a number of studies have explored this relationship between attractiveness and voice. These studies found that sound is key in determining whether we find someone attractive or not. Most women say they prefer men with deep voices, believing them to be stronger, more masculine. On a basic level they are the hunter/ gatherer that can best provide for a family. Men, on the other hand, find the higher-pitched voices of women the most attractive. It all boils down to hormones. When women produce more oestrogen their voices become slightly higher-pitched. Higher oestrogen levels also correlate with the point in the female cycle when they are closest to ovulation. So, on a basic level women are more attractive when they are most fertile, which won't exactly help you unless you wait until you ovulate each month before making or receiving calls. So how else can sound help us when we're communicating?

Well, attractive people were also said to sound the most confident. And although it may not be in our control to change the pitch of our voice, we can learn to sound more self-assured.

How to sound more confident

1 Slow down

Remember reading aloud in front of the whole class at school or delivering a presentation at work? When nerves kick in, unfortunately so does our vocal accelerator. We don't realise we're doing it either. Especially when it means we can shorten the time we have to stand there feeling embarrassed and awkward. Talking too fast is a clear sign you're nervous. We've mostly all felt it. Some people are just better at controlling their nerves than others.

Much of the reason for our 'sprint default' has to do the lifestyles we lead. We get everything now. We're like addicts hooked on instant gratification. We've forgotten how to wait and so we've largely lost the ability to temper our speed.

There's a solution to this though, and it's to do with the way we breathe. Fast lifestyles equal shallow breaths. Most of us are so used to this way of breathing that we no longer recognise how different, or beneficial, it feels to breath deeply. Taking deep, slow breaths is the best way to slow yourself down. Ever seen a stressed yogi? No. I rest my case.

Before you make or receive the call, take a deep breath. And another. And another… Aim to draw your breath in as if you're filling your abdomen from the bottom right up to your lungs. If it helps, visualise the air being drawn in and your diaphragm flattening to create more room. Imagine the muscles between your ribs expanding to make even more space.

Place a hand on your stomach while you're doing this – it should rise as you inhale and fall as you exhale. Stick with it and gradually, your inhales will become longer and deeper. Do this for two minutes before making your call. It will slow you down both mentally and physically not just for your phone call but generally.

Also, consciously slow down your speaking voice. Enunciate each word, speaking slowly and clearly. Practise it when you're alone. See how much you can slow your speech down. You won't be speaking to your date in this way, of course, but it does train you to speak in a more measured, controlled way.

2 *Vary your pace and pitch*

Speak in a monotone and you'll sound bored – of yourself, your subject matter and the person on the end of the phone. If you come across like this on the phone you'll have no hope of progressing to a date.

Have you ever noticed how television presenters use their body and gestures to animate their voice? If you naturally gesticulate when you speak, aim to do the same when you're talking on the phone. It will help your voice sound natural and bring some variation to your voice pitch. It's good to be a little animated. It shows you're interested in what you're talking about, passionate even, and it will reflect in your voice. Don't be so animated, of course, that you come across as hyperactive.

3 Avoid, like, the bad fillers...

We all use them. The 'ums' or 'ers' that show we're thinking about what to say next. They're quite normal in everyday conversation and unless you plan to launch a career as a public speaker they reflect the naturalness of your conversation.

It's the bad fillers, the bits of repetitive, meaningless slang you should avoid. I've had dates with men who've used 'like', 'you kow what I mean' and 'you get me though' way too much in conversation. You end up so distracted that you don't then hear what they're actually saying.

4 Think before you respond

We're generally quite unnerved by silence. It means we rush to fill the gaps in conversation, especially when we're talking to someone new, rather than taking the time to think about what we want to say. It's not our fault. It's been programmed into us from an early age that questions need answering – and quickly.

It's reinforced by so many things around us too. A while back, I was listening to a local radio station which was commemorating Remembrance Day. The presenter announced they were going to hold a minute's silence. But when it began it wasn't silent at all. It sounded like I was outside in the middle of a park. I could hear the sound of the wind in the trees, a distant plane and what sounded like the low buzz of nondescript white noise. This was the digital radio version of silence. Real silence on air potentially means lost listeners. Better, then that listeners are greeted with some sort of ambient sound if they happen to tune in. Actual silence would mean something was wrong. And it's sort of how we feel in real life. We're programmed to think silence is wrong and so we're uncomfortable with it. This means we don't give ourselves time to think. We respond just so there are no gaps in our conversation rather than take a few seconds to reflect on what we're being asked before we speak.

Confident speakers don't do this. They understand that it's ok to punctuate their conversations with silence. Confident speakers are happy to let the person they're talking to wait for their answer and think about what to say before they say it. Try it with a friend so it begins to feel more natural to you.

Confidence when speaking is all about slowing everything down – your pace, the way you answer, the way you speak. Manage this and you'll sound infinitely more comfortable.

9

Learning to listen

There's a difference between hearing someone and really listening to what they're saying. Quite often no real distinction is made, but to hear simply means to perceive sound. To listen is to absorb and comprehend what's being said.

The differences are subtle, but so often, we hear without actually listening. That's because we have our own agenda, regardless of the other person. That agenda consists of our own set of wants/needs and we're keen to tick each one off our imaginary list. If you hear someone you will comprehend their voice, their tone, whether it's soothing or whether it grates on you. But listen, I mean actually listen and you'll hear what someone is saying even if they don't actually say it. Consider the sentences below.

Are you wearing that tonight?
Are you wearing *that* tonight?

Yes, it's the same question. You can *hear* the same words being spoken. But if you *listen* and take notice of the stress applied to 'that' in the second example you learn more about what the speaker really feels about what you're going to be wearing that evening. And it isn't good. Rather than simply asking a question this person is suggesting you wear something else.

During a phone conversation with Terry who I'd met on a dating app, we were discussing what we were both looking for in a partner. One of the things on my list was someone with no drama. In response he asked, 'What no drama *whatsoever*?' adding significant stress to the final word. I replied with a laugh, assuming he was just making light of my statement. 'Well, as little as possible.' He laughed too and agreed he was looking for the same.

In our next conversation he was feeling low. When I asked if he was ok he told me about the difficult relationship he was having with his daughter and ex-partner; about an old school friend who was facing a prison term for fraud and the problems he was having at work. In other words: drama.

The thing is, I could see why he had agreed with me in our last conversation. His life was already filled with drama, so it stood to reason that he'd want a relationship that was relatively free of it. But if I'd listened, really listened, to his initial response in our first conversation – 'What, no drama *whatsoever*?' – it was my clue to what was really going on his life. He was telling me, however unwittingly, that his life was filled with drama.

In conversation, people tell you more about themselves than they often realise. But in many instances we hear only what we want to. So, when someone you're attracted to says, 'I'm not looking for a relationship right now' you assume he means with everyone else except you, because maybe, just maybe, you'll be the one to change his mind. So, instead of what he's actually saying you hear: 'Hang in there because if I fall for anyone it's going to be you'. And 'Looking for a bit of fun' becomes 'Yes, but I'll want to settle down once I get to know *you*'.

Thanks to the world wide web, we're asking for what we want in ways that weren't possible before. But we still choose to hear what we want to hear when we think we've found someone we like. We still attempt to make their dreams match ours, even if, in reality, we're poles apart. So, learn to listen to what the people you meet say. Don't hear what you want to. Those first couple of conversations will reveal a lot – if you listen. Don't let your ego take control.

An epic first conversation fail

I'd exchanged messages and emails with Tariq for two weeks before we spoke on the phone. He was already calling me 'babe' and 'sweetie', which was a little unnerving, and despite alarm bells ringing in the far reaches of my smitten mind I'd convinced myself it was a touching gesture. He asked for my telephone number.

Well, what he actually said was, 'Can I have your number because I'd really like to hear your voice.' He had potential and I guess it was making me feel full of the joys of spring (or more accurately, late winter…) and he had such a sweet smile in his profile pic that I tapped out my number and pressed send.

I got on with the rest of my day, certain I'd hear from him some time later. I imagined the conversation we'd have. I looked again at the interesting things in his profile ad and browsed his pictures. That smile… I was full of anticipation about that first call, wondering how his voice would sound, even jumping ahead of myself and visualising our first date. What I hadn't anticipated was that there'd be no phone call that day.

I assumed – no, made excuses that – he was busy at work. I understood because I was busy too. But when someone tells you they'd really like to hear your voice, you assume it's sometime soon.

A second day passed. A couple of times during the day, I wondered if he was going to call. Yes, I could have called him but I was hoping he'd be the kind of man to do what he said he would.

As the end of the third day approached I relunctantly began to wonder if I'd been ghosted, but he'd sounded genuinely interested so I didn't believe it was that. Whatever Tariq's reasons, by the fourth day I'd had enough. I shouldn't care, but I did. Expectation had dragged itself up behind me and hooked its claws in my back. I hated the fact I was feeling like a bunny boiler. This wasn't me. But how could I contact him without coming over all 'Glenn Close'. I had to find a way to confront the situation with some guarantee of success.

So, here's what I did. I sent him the following email:

Hello [I used his full name here, as it appeared in his email]. I have a very short multiple choice quiz for you… It really is VERY short and will take a few seconds of your time.

You haven't called the lady you met online. Is the reason for this…

a)   You've found the woman of your dreams and been swept off your feet

b)   You prefer a woman to take control – after all what was the point of the whole equality movement

c)   You have temporary amnesia and 'who the hell are you?'

d)   None of the above

See, very short, huh? Let me know your preferred answer.

It turned my anxiety into humour. It also gave me the chance to see where he was at by the answer he gave. I even alluded to the fact that I'd thought of calling him. A strange feeling of calm overcame me. I realised then that my anxiety was caused by my lack of control. As soon as he told me he was going to call I'd given away my power as I waited. I'd love to say it didn't matter if he responded, but I'd be lying. I wanted a reaction.

I sent the email off and, almost straightaway, I got a reply:

Baby [see what I mean] *this is a very funny quiz and you got me laughing so hard in the office today. Well, the answer is I didn't know you were a serious woman who was interested in me [duh!] as I was in you when I saw your profile. But now I think I know and am calling you NOW.*

And he did. Less than a minute later.

We'll get back to Tariq in a minute, but what soon became clear to me, is getting past the texting stage isn't always so straightforward. Sounding out someone through a conversation can reveal more about them than text messages and I found four types that never made it past the conversation stage for just this reason.

1 Hunk punks

Imagine. You're browsing through the endless list of faces on your phone when you glance someone who has you scrolling furiously backwards. He is magnificent: the kind of man that's everyone's version of Adonis. Your thumb hovers over his image before tapping it – partly because you think 'he'd never be interested in me'), partly because you know that once you've clicked it open he'll know you've checked him out and you'll have to deal with the fact he might not reciprocate.

You eventually overcome the self-doubt and tap his photo anyway. His profile unfolds like an exotic flower before you. You scroll through more glorious pictures. He's the right age, and has ticked a few of your boxes. But then you scroll down to the personal bit. The bit where he's supposed to give you an idea of what he's looking for; reveals a few things about himself; says something about who he is – anything. Instead of a few paragraphs there's just a row of xxxxxxxxxxxxxxxxxxxxxx.

I admit, I was drawn in by the images when I was first online. I'd skip right over the text phase, quite often at his insistence and onto the telephone, but in more cases than not he'd end up being a hunk punk.

On a hunk punk's profile you'll see one gorgeous photo after. He always looks hot or moody, is bare-chested and revealing a honed six-pack. He'll have muscles carved into areas of the body you didn't think possible, but as you scroll down the information giving you a sense of his personality will be patchy. I haven't quite figured it out but maybe they think they don't need to. It's understandable. They've rarely had to because their looks and physique do all the work for them. For most of their lives they've probably had members of the opposite sex dropping themselves at their feet. And if we manage to get with one of them we feel so lucky that our expectations are set pretty low.

Hunk punks tend not to fill in their profile ads because they've never really had to think about what other features might make them attractive to a potential match. You can't blame them really. Society likes to remind us of the 'perfect' man and woman.

None of the hunk punks I've met over the years had anything meaningful to say. Conversation with them was superficial and revolved around sexual innuendo and physical attraction.

2 Control freaks

This type wants to lead the conversation. Make all the decisions. He displays these things early on and they're not difficult to spot. There's nothing wrong with showing a bit of initiative. I like a man who is happy to decide where we meet for a date, what activity we could do. But control freaks display an extreme level of control.

Cliff lived locally to me and suggested we talk early on in our communication. He was a pro at this game – or so he said. He'd been on and off dating websites for four years and understood the importance of moving things along. His messages were clever, but hinted at a playful nature. When he called we spoke for a few minutes, while we tuned into each other's voices. As we chatted I began to feel thirsty so walked into the kitchen as we talked to get a glass of water.

'What are you doing?' said Cliff, in what I assumed was mock seriousness.

'Just pouring myself a drink,' I said.

'Well it would be great to have your full attention,' he said. 'I mean I'm sitting here talking to you, not allowing myself to be distracted by anything; listening to your every word…'

'Are you kidding?' I said, interrupting his flow.

He wasn't. But tried to make light of it when I asked him why getting a drink bothered him so much.

He laughed it off and asked instead if I had children. I told him I had a daughter. I was surprised he'd asked because it was very clearly stated on my profile. I wondered if he'd read it. Our conversation stalled and I imagined bundles of tumbleweed rolling around in digital space. Then he said, 'I never normally date women with children.'

'Why's that?' I said.

'Well…' he said. 'Imagine you start dating someone with three kids. You're always going to be fourth in the pecking order. You're never going to be their main focus.'

I thought about it before replying. 'But don't you put your son first?' I asked. (Yes, I had read *his* profile).

He mumbled and said yes.

'So, how's it different?' I wasn't being facetious. I genuinely wanted to know why it was okay for him but not for a woman.

His answer was mumbled and incoherent and he quickly

changed the subject. "So, I thought we could meet nearer me as I'm not too far from you. I know this little café that I often take first dates to. It's just around the corner from the station and there's no parking restrictions so I can comfortably park. It's a cool place. Tuesday's good for me. Shall we say around 6.30pm?'

That was when I checked out. Completely. When I tuned into his words he was making it very clear that he wasn't interested in anyone other than himself. Everything about his plan for our date was about making things convenient for him. I was an afterthought, just the woman lucky enough to be his latest date. He assumed I was happy to travel to him, that I was available on Tuesday at 6.30pm and that I wanted to go with him to a café he 'often' took first dates to. The fact he had the gall to tell me would have been hilarious if he wasn't so clueless. I actually began to feel a little sorry for him. Shortly afterwards I brought the conversation to a close. And, no, he didn't get past the 'talk' stage.

3 Dodgy dudes

I'm not talking fraudsters here. They're far too clever and charming to be caught out at the conversation stage. No. I'm referring to those people who have something else going on that isn't above board. Let's return to the conversation with Tariq. We left him, having just replied to my carefully worded multiple choice email. Here's what happened next…

As soon as I answered the phone, things went downhill. Fast.

'Where did you get my full name?' he demanded.

'What do you mean?' I said.

'I didn't tell you my full name.'

I explained that it was in all the emails he'd sent me and that he sounded suspicious. I wondered whether my email quiz, however carefully worded, had still somehow screamed bunny boiler.

Added to this my phone signal kept coming and going and Tariq had to call me back two more times before complaining about it and telling me to call him back instead. Maybe he's having a bad day I thought, even though I didn't believe it. I called him back, tried to resume a normal conversation. I asked him where he was from. 'The US,' he said with an accent anything but American.

'Really,' I said, 'you don't sound very American. Did you grow up somewhere else?' It seemed an innocent enough question.

'Why are you asking where I'm from? I don't really want to talk about that until I know who you are,' he said.

What the hell??? I thought. Alarm bells were hammering in my ears, so I gave in. 'I think from some of the things you've said, we're not right for each other so…'

Before I finished the sentence Tariq cursed down the phone at me, then hung up.

Dodgy Dudes are cagey. They may avoid answering your questions, or ask you why you're asking any at all. Considering the reason you're talking to them in the first place is so you can find out more about them, their behaviour will come across as odd. Suspicious people are generally hiding something. It's up to you whether you stick around long enough to find out what it is.

4 Open liars

At some point you may decide to widen your search parameters. Sherrill, a friend of mine, was the first to suggest it. She'd been online for a while before she decided that the chances of finding Mr Right within the confines of the M25 might not be the most sensible option. And it makes sense. Who knows where he'll be? So, she extended her search to 100 miles of home. That's when she met Tony and six years in they're happily married.

It was simple, perfect logic. So the next time I was online I extended my search to 150 miles. Within days, I met Lucas. He lived in Birmingham and one of the first things he said in his message was he wasn't sure about starting a long-distance relationship. I said it was cool. You get to a point when you're dating online, when you stop putting all your hopes into one possible suitor. So, I was happy to chat for a while then let it fizzle out. But, despite this, Lucas stayed in contact, sending texts out of the blue.

According to his profile he had no children, but during one of our early conversations he mentioned he was going to be taking his son to football at the weekend.

'But, your profile says you don't have any children,' I said.

'Oh that…' he said. 'No one is honest on their profile.'

'I am,' I replied.

It was the first time I'd met someone who thought like that. He believed that your profile was just a marketing tool that you used simply to get yourself noticed. He believed you'd get around to the truth if, or when, it was relevant.

He was pretty open about it, so I gave him the benefit of

the doubt. Gradually he fessed up about the other aspects of his profile that were fake. His job, where he lived… He was charming and funny and even though his ability to lie so matter-of-factly didn't sit well with me we continued to talk.

I had a work booking up in Birmingham a couple of weeks into our conversations so I decided to test him. I suggested it might be a good opportunity for us to meet and he agreed. We arranged to meet the following Thursday. On Wednesday, he called to say he wasn't sure he'd be able to make our meeting – he'd been asked to go on a business trip to Manila in the Phillipines that morning.

It was a stretch too far. Even if he really was going to South America I knew I'd never be able to trust him.

I stopped communicating with him when I realised he was too scared to actually meet. Maybe he was married, in a relationship or playing games. The point was: if lying was so easy for him how would I ever know when he was telling the truth?

What about the good guys?

You'll chat to many men you'll say ciao to before you ever get to meet them. Then, after a few phone conversations, there'll be the men who have impressed you enough to go out on a date. Goodbye virtual world, hello physical one…

Step Three

Date

10

Date Expectations

Confession time. Before I tried online dating I'd only ever had two dates. Both of which were in my teens and way before the internet was let loose on the world. The first was with the friend of a friend who admitted he'd liked me from afar for at least a year before he found the courage to ask me out. It was unexpected and flattering because he was cute, in a quiet sort of way. We went to a movie – I can't remember which one – and afterwards he drove me home. Our conversation was stilted. By inexperience, nerves or both. When I said goodnight he leaned over to kiss me and our teeth clashed. We looked at each other and laughed, both agreeing that maybe this was a sign. We were better as friends. It was easy. No one was forced into that uncomfortable place where you had to make the other person feel rejected or awkward. I didn't have to let him down and vice versa.

The second was a blind date with the brother of a friend. I was nervous and worried in equal measure. At least with date number one I'd met him, knew what he looked like, had chatted and got to know each other as friends before our date. But, what if I didn't like this man? How would I let him down? What would I say to my friend? I tried to create as many scenarios in my head as I could to help me prepare for the inevitably bad experience I was going to have. I was curious, yes, but also sure we wouldn't get on. Maybe because of this, the date went exceptionally well. Our conversation felt natural and easy, he was attractive and funny, relaxed and cool. When the date came to a close we agreed to see each other again. It was the start of a relationship that lasted 16 years and saw him become my husband and the father of our child. I guess you could say it remains my most successful date ever, however inexperienced I was back then, and despite the divorce that eventually followed many years later.

The thing with both these dates, though, is neither gave me the opportunity to practice saying no. And when I re-entered the dating scene in my late thirties (and then my late forties) this was one of my single biggest concerns. I wasn't comfortable with confrontation, preferring to find compromise or agreeing to disagree. Back then I worried too much about what people thought or about hurting their feelings. When it came to dates, how would

I tell someone I wasn't interested? When would I tell them? At the end of the date? Afterwards? By phone? By text?

But a bigger concern was how to cope with the rejection I'd feel when someone wasn't interested in me. How to manage that feeling of disappointment or the belief I'd never find someone that was a good fit. It took me a while to understand that there was no point questioning why someone thinks you're not right for them. The best thing you can do for yourself is accept it and move on. When you go on lots of dates, you learn a lot. Lessons about people, about the process and about yourself. After a while you learn that rejection is an unavoidable part of dating. It will also begin to have less of an impact on you.

Virtually real

So you've found someone who's survived both the text and talk stages. From this point on it's all about meeting in the flesh and seeing whether that hint of chemistry you felt truly exists, or whether the whole thing has been one massive chemical reaction gone wrong. This is the part that takes you out of the virtual world and back to the physical one. It's also where you find out if you both look the way you say you do, how compatible you are and whether you'll want to see each other again. It's the game changer. Or, more accurately, the game developer. Hopefully you've taken heed of all the signs so far and not allowed yourself to get too carried away or attached so that if things don't quite go to plan it'll be easy to extract yourself from the situation.

My first ever date with a man I'd met online didn't lead to everlasting love. Not that it can't, it's just, realistically, you're better off thinking of it as practise – especially, when you've been off the dating scene for some time. Go into it with the idea that you're just going to enjoy meeting countless new people and if anything more serious develops it's a welcome bonus.

I wish I'd known that before my first date. When you haven't dated for many years (or ever!), there's one big problem. It's something you bring with you that you have no idea you're carrying: expectation.

Great (or not so great) expectations…

Think about the most recent blockbuster movie you've seen that ended up disappointing you. Most likely, before you saw it everywhere you went: at home, at work, on the bus or in the press – friends, journalists or randoms on the street were talking about it. You may have heard snippets about the most captivating scenes; or a cinematic technique the director used; or the film's most tear-jerking or funny moment. The critics have given it four or five stars and there's such a general social buzz about it, you're almost a social pariah if you haven't seen it. All of this is building your expectation, building your excitement for the day you'll get to see it. But when you eventually book tickets, buy the popcorn and settle yourself in your premier seat, the film has already lost. There's no way it can come close to all the comments you've heard. You sit back in your seat waiting to feel stirred. To feel that same level of exhilaration everyone else has. But you never quite get there. You leave the cinema wondering what all the fuss was about.

Movie blockbuster or potential boyfriend: it's a horrible thing expectation. We imagine what it's going to be like when we meet them. We picture how they'll look in real life, whether they'll match their photo, how we're going to feel, whether we'll sit opposite or next to them, where we'll go, what we'll do. We build a picture in our minds of just how we want the date to go. Our excitement fuels our thoughts and on some level we begin to believe that what we've imagined is how it'll be in reality.

It won't. You see, our expectation is that this person could be our next long-term partner or husband. At 50 plus we're looking for that person we can share a fulfilling second-wind life with. It means we end up applying unnecessary pressure to a situation that should be fun. Expectation is a bummer.

How to side-step expectations

✓ **Don't believe the hype.** Whatever your date has told you about themselves it's up to you to see if they are who they say they are. So don't get excited. Remember, when you meet their actions will tell you more about them than anything they've said. All you have to do is pay attention.

✓ **Don't daydream about what the date will be like.** Imagining it will be perfect will ensure that it isn't. Focus on events you have in your diary in for the day after, on a night out with a girlfriend or on your plans for the weekend.

✓ **Will you feel the same when you meet?** However connected you feel while you've been messaging or when you've spoken on the phone, remind yourself that you may not feel the same in person.

✓ **Imagine what it would be like if you don't get on**. Decide how you'd deal with it and what you might say. This kind of thinking will ground you and balance your thoughts.

11

Dating etiquette

We all think it, but no one wants to talk about it. At least not before the date. It's one of those sensitive questions that is usually avoided, right up until the moment the bill is slapped down on its silver saucer with the accompanying complimentary mints. The question is: **who should pay?** I posed the question in a blog poll a while back and 52% said the pair should go Dutch, 45% said it was the man's responsibility to pay and 3% said it was the woman's prerogative. So feminism, it seems, has evened out the playing field.

I've had dates with men who insist on paying even when I've offered to contribute, men who've 'forgotten' their wallets and men happy to go half. Here's an easy solution. If the man asks you out he pays. If you ask him, you pay. Go Dutch from date two.

Interestingly, psychologists say that if a man insists on paying, he's showing you he has the means to look after you. He wants to make you feel secure and that if you enter a relationship with him he'll be able to support you. So, if he insists don't quibble about it. Just enjoy the free meal.

The things we hide - two approaches

1 To say...

On our first date Wayne smiled a wide, full smile as he walked up to me. The first physical thing I noticed was his teeth. They were a little uneven and discoloured, but he had such a vibrant, cool energy about him that I really didn't care. My attention had been piqued by his profile ad so I hadn't paid too much attention to the detail in his photos. But on reflection, I realised he'd used the technique I mentioned earlier – he'd gone for the moody, closed-mouth look in all four of his pictures.

When we sat down to have a drink, he decided to bring the topic up in conversation. He explained why he'd opted not to have work done to fix them. He explained that they reflected who he was now and that it was just his particular imperfection. We all had them. He was right, of course. It was such an honest and brave way to broach a subject he was acutely conscious of that it endeared me to him even more.

2 Or not to say...

When a friend of mine was dating, she decided to meet up with a man she'd been talking to for two weeks. She arrived first, was shown to a table and sat down to wait. He arrived a few minutes later and as he approached she noticed a lump on his right temple about the size of a cherry tomato. As they greeted each other and he sat down, she wondered why she hadn't noticed the lump in any of his pictures. She thought back and realised for the first time that in all of the three pictures she'd seen of him he'd been standing or sitting with his face set to the side.

He didn't mention it and neither did she and so it became the 'tomato' in the room. He knew it was there, she knew it was there, but no one dared go near it. And, of course, in that way you do when you discover something you weren't expecting she couldn't take her eyes off it, which made her (and probably him) feel even more uncomfortable. Although their phone conversations had been interesting and fun, the conversation now was stilted and lacked flow. Both parties were now feeling ill at ease and it had spilled over into the way they were interacting with each other. At the end of an awkward night, they parted ways.

Telling it like it is

Above are two different approaches to a similar problem: how to reveal something you're uncomfortable with. Someone in control and someone who let the situation control him. The key thing here is how the approach we take makes us feel. Tackle it head on and you'll feel more confident. You decide when and where and how you tell your date. As Wayne said in the first example, we all have imperfections. It's what makes us interesting. But we've been brought up in a world obsessed by perfection. We're surrounded by images of the 'perfect' body, the 'perfect' partner, the 'perfect' date as though these ideals are the only realistic goals. As women, we're taught about finding 'Mr Right' from before we can walk. He's in fairytales, in cartoons, in the movies. We carry these preconceptions with us into our adult lives. We're looking for him, even if we don't think we are. But we're forgetting a key thing. We're not perfect. And neither is he.

It's not easy to be open about something you're conscious of. But whether it's a birthmark, a bald patch or a few extra pounds the big reveal *will* happen. All you have to do is decide whether you want to be in control of when it does or suffer the awkwardness, discomfort or even disdain that can follow when you're exposed.

Talk to anyone who's dated online and they'll have an anecdote about someone they've met who is either way older than their picture, carrying more weight or who looked like a different person to the one pictured on their profile. It's a common problem.

Don't become someone's witty dating story.

If you're brave enough to do what Wayne did, you'll be taking control of when and how you talk about whatever it is you feel uncomfortable with. And we all like to be the master of our own destiny. Think about what you'll say. Practise it on a friend and get their feedback. Then practise it again. Remember, if your date is put off by what you say during a phone conversation, they won't react any differently to it in person. They'll dislike you more, though, for not being upfront about it beforehand.

Added to this, the fact you're hiding something (however small it might be) is going to make you feel anxious, before and during the date. Before you meet, you fret about how the person will react when they see you, which means you won't be relaxed. You'll also spend the whole time you're there trying to figure out what they really think about you. And there'll be no way of knowing for sure – which will cause you even more anxiety. It won't be an enjoyable experience for you or them.

Follow the 90/10 conversation rule

I don't believe there's any topic you can't touch on during a first date. But there are some things you should definitely just touch and not go into in any great depth. It's okay to mention exes or what you're looking for in a partner, just give more emphasis to getting to know your date instead. Use the 90/10 rule. Aim to focus 90 per cent of the conversation on getting to know your partner, having fun and enjoying whatever it is you've decided to do. Allow just 10 per cent of your time together to touch on some of those bigger topics – if that. But don't dwell on them.

We're all different, but one thing you don't want to do is give the impression you're bitter and/or living in the past. If all goes well, this is hopefully the first of many dates. You're leaving the past behind you. So start now. A first date isn't the time or place to dig up weeds. It's about planting and cultivating new seeds. Mentioning that you and your ex broke up because you wanted different things isn't the same as be-moaning their lying/cheating ways for the first hour of your date.

Good conversation, chemistry and attraction will lead to some satisfying dates. But there will be times when you're not compatible.

And for these you'll have to tell them you're not interested.

Saying thanks, but no thanks

You can feel yourself gradually wilting as the date rolls on. You're not feeling him, even though he seems oblivious to the fact. You get to the end of the date and he asks you how you think it's gone. You hope he hasn't noticed you visibly wince. But how do you tell him you're not interested? Letting someone down isn't easy. So what do you do? There are four approaches you'll need to consider:

1 Be honest

We're back to one of my three key principles. But is it the best policy when you have to let someone down? Is there ever a good way to be honest about the fact you're not interested? Brutal honesty isn't easy to deliver or receive. We've all been on the receiving end of this kind of let down and we remember how it feels. The thing is, honesty is easy when we're being complimentary, not so when we have to explain why someone isn't right for us. But regardless of all this, it *is* still the best policy. Your date will be clear that things will go no further and they'll know why.

If your date asks how you think the date went at the end of the evening, this is the time to be honest. But keep it short and be kind. Always say something you enjoyed about the date first, then follow up succinctly with why don't want to see them again.

2 Do it later

If you're too nervous or uncomfortable to do it in person, let them know later by text or phone. Some people believe it's cowardly but as we've seen we communicate more by text than we do by phone so times have changed. It's still also *far* better than saying nothing. You've both invested time writing and talking to each other so you owe it to them to tell them something.

A follow-up text or phone call after the date, just to say thank you should be standard, whether you're interested or not. So use it to tell them how you feel. You can still be honest and kind in your word choices, and again keep it short. You could even preempt it be apologizing for not having the guts to do it in person, but that you thought it was still better than 'ghosting' them. They'll quietly thank you for it. Which moves me onto the next item on the list…

3 'Ghost' them

It's rude. There's no other way to dress this up. Disappearing without a trace, when you've been communicating, or been on a date, with someone shows them no respect. Now that we're increasingly using apps to find dates, something about their immediacy, or the flippant way we can swipe through potential partners gives many free license to treat people as nothing more than pixels on a screen.

There are reasons why people choose this option though. They might not be good with confrontation, unable to face hurting your feelings in person or suffering from anxiety or depression. Some are married or in relationships and have had some kind of personal 'wake up' call to stop them in their tracks. Others are chatting to so many others that you slip through their massive net.

In extreme cases, people have 'ghosted' dates when they've felt threatened. Some people don't accept kind rejection. Instead they hear: '*I could be interested though, if you try harder*'. They'll keep sending messages, become obsessed or even end up stalking someone. But be warned, ghosting them can also feed their obsession.

If you do decide to do this, think about how you'd feel if someone you liked did it to you. Sure, you get over it, but not without wasting your time sending texts and messages over the next few days until the realisation slowly dawns.

4 Enter the friend zone

If you're genuine about wanting to stay friends, this is a gentler way to exit the dating zone. There are people who have developed lasting friendships as the result of a date gone awry. But if you're using it to soften the blow, you're effectively keeping the lines of communication open with someone you'd rather not.

There's always one person who's more into the other. For them, entering the friend zone is a waiting game: they're waiting for you to change your mind. Then there's attraction. You were attracted to each other enough to go out on that first date. So what happens to that sexual attraction when you become friends? Friends with benefits are cool when you're both single and unattached. But how are they going to feel when you go out on other dates, meet someone, fall in love? How will you feel if the situation is reversed? Ask yourself these questions: do you really need more friends? What's the friendship based on: shared interests, humour, careers? If you know they're still attracted to you, won't this just give them false hope?

Be honest with yourself and, then, be honest with them.

10 lessons in 10 dates

12

The things you learn

One of my friends described me as a patient dater. It's probably true. I had roughly 150 first dates and although some were unforgettable and others awful, I did try to give each the benefit of the doubt. You learn a lot about yourself, the more men you meet. You also begin to get a clear sense of what you're looking for in a partner. So here follows 10 dates I learnt lessons from. Like many good lessons in life, some simply reinforced what I already new, others made me re-think what I wanted. So here goes…

1 The 'bitter' one

I met Warren at London's Waterloo station, outside the M&S. This was my first. The first time I'd agreed to a date with someone I'd met online. The excitement I'd felt that morning had transfomed into anxiety by afternoon as my head filled with questions I had no way of answering: What if I like him? What if I don't? How will I tell him? How will I escape?

At just before 6pm I left work with, what I thought was, ample time but still managed to rock up a few minutes late – one of those errors in judgement that comes from working too close to the meeting point.

It was early winter but the cold was already biting. As I walked up, Warren blew hot air into his cupped hands. He was smaller than me in my 3in heels, and significantly shorter than I remembered from his profile stats. He also looked different. But, then, there was no sign of the Cheshire-cat grin he wore in his profile picture: a grin so wide it had consumed half of his face.

'Hey,' I say.

'Hi. *I* got here early,' he said, emphasising the 'I'. And that's when he did it for the very first time. He sniggered. A nervous, 'I-don't-know-what-else-to-do-but-snigger' kind of snigger.

I was nervous too, which resulted in a case of conversational diarrhoea. I could feel I was doing it but couldn't stop. I began to feel like this date was a bad idea. We decided to walk along the Southbank to find somewhere to have a drink. As we walked he sniggered and I chattered. It wasn't the best combination. We found a pub away from the river and he bought us drinks. I stayed off the alcohol, worried that my patter would go up a notch.

We sat at a table near the bar. Before long the conversation turned to past relationships. A big first date no-no according to 'they'. But my date either didn't know the rules or he didn't care. Instead he stomped around the no man's land as if he was gunning for the enemy. 'She was selfish... she was always out with her mates... she was untidy... she... she... she...'

I tuned out.

I was feeling hungry so when he eventually paused – to snigger – I suggested we go for something to eat. We found a Thai noodle place that looked good, judging by the queue. While we were waiting he stared at me and smiled. I asked him what was wrong. 'Nothing,' he said, 'I'm just looking at the height thing.'

I was tempted to say, 'Yeah, the height thing you neglected to mention,' but I decided to let him have his moment.

It was one of those 'sit, eat, leave' street food restaurants where you're led to tables banked by long benches, then wedged between two sets of strangers. Unless, of course, the waiter has your back and sticks you at the end of a table. But the waiter wasn't on our side that night and when we shuffled into our vacant patches on each bench and started chatting, it was clear the couples either side of us had sussed it was a first date, especially when one guy leaned across and winked at Warren.

Then I forgot where I was and why I was there (or maybe it was a subconscious decision) and ordered noodles. Bloody noodles. The messiest, most embarrassing thing a woman can eat on a first date. You try getting a forkful into your mouth without spraying sauce everywhere.

As I slurped my noodles he slagged off his past dates. 'She was fat, she was depressed, she was too full on… she… she… she…

A strange feeling of déjà vu overcame me.

He really wasn't selling himself that well. But then – when I imagined myself sitting where he was watching me tackle the tangled mess on my plate – neither was I.

So, it's a surprise when he suddenly said, 'Well, just the first kiss to tackle now.'

I almost choked. But after a split-second vision of him performing the Heimlich manoeuvre on me, the rogue noodle slipped eagerly down my throat.

'First kiss?' I said.

He sniggered.

I asked for the bill.

Strangely enough on the way back to the station he was full of the joys of a successful first date. At the top of the escalator he leaned in for a kiss. I shook my head and then his hand. 'Thanks for a nice evening,' I said, 'But let's just leave it there shall we?'

LESSON: DON'T BAD MOUTH YOUR EXES

There's nothing wrong with talking about exes, but never bad mouth them. What happened to you is in the past. If you're still feeling bitter, lay off the dating for a while. Put yourself in the place of your date. Is it going to endear them to you? No. Will you sound negative? Yes. Will they run a mile? Hell, yes.

2 The 'available' one

I finally arrange a date with Samir. We'd spoken once, texted a few times but hadn't quite managed to meet. To be honest, with all the missed opportunities I'd ruled him out. So, when I get an impromptu text from him asking if I'm free that night I think, 'What the hell' and I agree to meet. His heritage is mixed but he refers to himself as Moroccan. He's 10 years my junior. So, I'm a cougar. It's official.

We meet at London Bridge. I arrive first, but don't have to wait long. He rushes up looking just like his profile picture and I guess, because he's recognized me, I must do too. He's tall, dressed well and has an intense face that softens when he smiles. He greets me with a kiss on the cheek and starts walking. Fast. Now, I'm a fast walker but Samir he's got the whole 'quick pace' thing licked. He walks like a man who knows where the journey's going to end.

'So you've got a place in mind?' I say. He nods and explains that it's a Thai restaurant not far from the station. Within minutes we're there. The restaurant is busy, but there's a table by the wall so Samir strides over to secure it.

Dinner is fine, if a little bland, but the conversation is vibrant. Samir asks if I'm bothered about the age gap. I tell him it's not something I'd noticed. Time passes quickly, the way it does when you're enjoying yourself. The chemistry is good. He sprinkles a few compliments my way. We talk. We laugh. We move onto a bar.

When we've got drinks and have settled into one of the bar's comfy leather sofas we talk about what we're looking for.

I tell him I'm just dating at the moment, that I'm seeing what's out there and that I'm not ready for anything serious. He's ready for a relationship and if he finds someone he gels with he'll focus on developing it.

That's when our discussion turns serious. Samir tells me I'm going through what he calls a 'selfish' phase. 'You're out there dating, meeting people who potentially want to start a relationship, but you're not ready to settle down, so it's all about you.'

He made me think. Was I being selfish? I knew what I wanted and where I was at, but hadn't really thought about what anyone else might want. I wonder where all this is coming from.

'Where's all this coming from,' I say.

'I'm just talking hypothetically,' he says. 'I've been there. I've done the whole 'selfish' thing and people get hurt.'

And then it dawns on me. Maybe I was being selfish. But on reflection, so was he. He was ready to start a relationship with the right person and didn't want to compromise that by simply dating. But isn't that where all relationships start?

The problem was there was chemistry between us, he's available, but my commitment to a relationship isn't. It's way too early in the dating game for me to consider starting a new relationship. We're stuck in our own selfish ruts.

But there's also something else to consider. As a younger man, Samir has time to spend a year or two exploring the possibilities of a relationship that may not work. I don't feel I have the same luxury. I want to be in a relationship that has a good chance of going the distance. I also need to feel ready, and just now I'm not.

'So basically what you're saying,' he continues. 'Is we won't see each other again. That's kind of what you mean if you say you're just dating.'

It actually isn't what I'm saying, but it's obviously what he's decided he needs to hear so I don't argue the point. The fire in our conversation does something to us both and Mr M leans in to kiss me. It's nice.

It really would be good to have a second date, but reluctantly I have to admit that he's right – it would be the kind of selfish act that wouldn't do either of us any good.

LESSON: IT'S OK TO BE SELFISH

Everyone comes to the table with their list of wants in a partner. And with the vast choices online we have a good chance of getting what we want. Selfishness in dating terms is about learning what will work for you and what won't. Sometimes that might be very different from that person you've just met and like. Recognise where you are in the process and respect it. If you're not ready for a relationship, that's cool. When the time's right, you'll find someone who's at the same stage as you.

3 The 'old-fashioned' one

Before we meet I learn that Devon is an engineer; that he describes himself as an old-fashioned gent'; that he admires 'strong' women and that he's been married – twice. Our first conversation was two hours long, whiling away the time it took him to drive to his night shift in Berkshire. By the time I put the phone down I was confident that he showed real potential.

He arrives first and, thanks to traffic, I wander in a few minutes later. The waitress at the door shows me to the back of the restaurant and as I approach the corner table a man stands up. He's wearing too baggy jeans with a shirt half tucked in. Ok, so while I'm not the fashion police you *are* on a date. At least decide whether the shirt should be out or in. I can feel myself giving him that once over – you know when your eyes do the whole head to toe thing and the result isn't good. Worse still, I think he notices. But the bigger problem is he doesn't really look like his profile pic. There's a vague resemblance, yes, but his face is fuller. Much fuller. Like he's eaten one too many pies.

I'm sounding shallow, I know. I'd be a fool to try to deny it. But to my point. Posting old photos of yourself when your appearance has significantly changed is a LIE. And we all know that's not the best way to start anything.

I sit down anyway, prepared to give Devon the benefit of the doubt. And actually the conversation starts off well. We pick up where our phone chats ended and the conversation flows effortlessly. Then he throws in a corker. 'Has anyone ever told you,

you might be a bit daunting?' he says. I ask him what he means. 'Well, you've got a great job, your own place, you know what you want…"

'But surely those are good things,' I say.

'Well… yes, but a guy can feel that you don't really need him,' he says.

I look back at him, blankly as he stumbles on. 'I mean… if I think of most of the guys I know, they haven't achieved what women like you have. Or if they've had it in the past they don't have it now.'

I feel like I've been punched in the belly. And that's when I realise. We'd enjoyed great chats on the phone. I'd been drawn in by our conversations, and was excited when we eventually arranged the date. EXPECT-ing the perfect connection. EXPECT-ing to be bowled over in person. EXPECT-ing to skip off into the sunset surrounded by that love glow. But Devon had reminded me why I should have left my expectations at home.

'So, do you feel daunted by me?' I say out of curiosity.

He pauses. 'Yeah, I guess so,' he says.

I don't really know what to say, so I say nothing. The rest of the meal passes with the kind of small talk no one remembers. As we're waiting for the bill, Devon looks across the table at me. 'Well, I think it would be good to see each other again.'

I open my mouth to reply but am interrupted by the waitress with the bill. Devon either thinks I agree or decides its best not to let me speak at all.

'Now, I'm not sure what you want to do about this,' he says. 'I'm more than happy to pay, but I've been on three dates now and paid for the first two, so it would be great if we can go Dutch.'

I dig out my card, definitely not wanting to owe him anything. We get up to leave and he marches off, opening the restaurant door and closing it behind him – in front of me. So much for being an old-fashioned gent… Outside, surprisingly, he's waiting for me. 'So, it would be good to see you again," he reiterates. I look back at him and in that second there is an understanding between us.

'Thanks, but it's not going to work for me,' I say.

LESSON: LET THEM SHOW NOT TELL

When people tell you who they are, it's only part of the picture. Our early conversations are filled with nerves and expectations, questions and assumptions – there's a lot going on. We're sussing out the best way to sell ourselves and gauging the kind of person they are. If we're really interested we'll tell them the things we think they want to hear and sometimes even stretch the truth a little. It's why, when you meet in person, you need to tune in to their actions to complete the picture. People show you who they are without realising it. Devon, who told me he liked strong women, was daunted by someone he perceived as successful. He described himself as an old-fashioned gent then quibbled over the bill and let himself out of the door, without a backward glance. Both of which were at odds with how he described himself. His words told me one thing, while his actions showed quite the opposite.

4 The 'best date ever' one

'It's going to be the best first date you've ever had."

I remember the evening Patrick said this. It was midsummer and I was sitting in my kitchen with the back door open looking out at the garden as we chatted on the phone. We'd been in contact via emails and texts for three weeks. He'd suggested two dates in that time, but I'd genuinely been busy on both nights. Now, in the last couple of days, we'd agreed on a day and time that suited us both.

A couple of days before our date, Patrick sent me a selection of pictures that weren't on his profile. He was playing tennis in one, in another he looked as if he was making a speech in front of an audience and in a third he was wearing a bright green T-shirt, cycling helmet and Lycra shorts and he was sat on a horse. It was in this, the third picture that he looked way, way older than in any of his other pictures. I wondered about that picture over the next day or so. I had a gut feeling that this was how he looked now. But we'd gotten on well on the phone and so still wanted to see how we'd get on in person.

On the morning of the date he called three times to check I was still okay to meet and to put the time of the date back a little. Eventually, I made my way to our meeting point. He called as I was coming up the escalator to let me know he would be a few minutes late, so when I arrived I leant against the wall and waited. I'm never sure of which I prefer most – arriving early and watching your date walking up to you or getting there second, knowing they're watching you approach.

But with Patrick it was neither of the above – instead he sidled up without me noticing, until I felt a tap on my arm. I looked up into his face. He looked older than the horse picture and sported a sheen of light perspiration on his brow. But that wasn't what struck me the most. In one hand he was balancing his bicycle and after a quick scan I could see he was wearing the knee-high Lycra shorts, helmet and T-shirt he had in the horse photo. We gave each other an awkward hug, made more awkward by the bike, before he launched into a trickle of conversation about everything he had planned for the date. We were going to have a picnic. The Thames was at low tide, revealing just a touch of beach and he'd prepared a light lunch. It was a beautiful idea – for a second or third date. A thoughtful, romantic gesture that's perfect once you've met and established how you get on in person. But it's a risky call for a first date. When you haven't met someone, especially if you've stretched the truth a bit about who you really are, you risk wasting time and effort on a date that could easily go either way.

When we got to the beach, Patrick rolled out a square of lino. [Yes. Lino]. Instead of a punnet of strawberries he'd brought a whole plant with two ripe strawberries he'd grown himself. He'd even brought his guitar to serenade me. But it all felt too much too soon and any chemistry that might have been there over the phone hovered just out of reach – like that feeling you get when you're trying to remember something on the tip of your tongue.

Patrick took out two plastic Champagne flutes and containers filled with a kedgeree dish he'd made especially. He apologised for the stickiness of the cups, saying 'they had been clean when I put the basket on top of the cupboard last year'. It didn't bode well.

We sat on the lino, with cups in hand. Further along the tiny beach a four-piece band were playing for the crowds up on the walkway who were peering over the rail and throwing money down in appreciation. I began to feel like a zoo exhibit. He said he loved coming here, and I really wanted to agree but as I watched the brown water lap up, trimmed with floating debris, I wanted to be anywhere but here. He'd gone to so much trouble I felt awful that I didn't feel the same. So I stayed so as not to spoil his moment.

At the end of the date, Patrick asked me how I think it'd gone. I told him that although I really appreciated all the trouble he'd gone to, I think we could both agree it hadn't quite worked out.

He looked at me blankly and said he felt entirely the opposite.

LESSON: KEEP FIRST DATES SIMPLE

First dates are all about chemistry. We want is to know if it's there in person. What you don't want is to be stuck in a hot air balloon high over the Cotswolds, with champers and chocolates, if the chemistry evaporates when you meet in the flesh. First dates aren't about going overboard to impress. They're about an introduction and about being authentic. And those are best done without the frills – however strongly you feel you've connected with a person. So if a date suggests something elaborate first time round, suggest keeping it simple. There'll be time for theatrics later. Better to underwhelm and impress than overwhelm and disappoint.

5 The 'drunk' one

The date with Mark started well. He'd booked us a table at a restaurant and I hadn't been waiting long before he strolled up. He was wearing a rain mac with long sleeves that almost entirely covered his hands and hung loosely on his body.

He hailed a cab and the driver laughed when he mentioned the name of the restaurant which, he said, was five-minutes away on foot. 'Well, at least let me impress the lady," said Mark, winking at me and guiding me into the back of the cab.

Two minutes later we were outside the restaurant. Inside, a wall of windows sat opposite a row of decadent white pillars. Glistening chandeliers hung at intervals all the way to the far wall. Chocolate brown chairs and sofas defined the bar area and beyond the pillars dining tables were laid out in immaculate rows.

We were early so after taking my coat – Mark decided he wanted to keep his mac on – we were shown into the bar area where we'd wait until our table was ready. Mark passed me the cocktail menu. Across six pages, a comprehensive list of familiar and unusual cocktails stretched before us. We laughed at some of the names, wondered at some of the combinations and eventually settled on our choices. When our drinks arrived, Mark took a sip then complained that he couldn't taste any alcohol in his and immediately called the waiter over to complain. His drink was topped up with another shot of rum and we were shown to our table. As we neared the table the waitress again asked Mark if she could take his mac. Again, he refused. Mark sat down and leant forward, pushing his coat sleeves back. 'You look great,' he said.

I thanked him and we scanned the menus. Our waiter came over to take our drink order. 'Let's get a bottle of wine,' said Mark. 'You ok with that?' I nodded.

'I'll let the lady choose,' he told the waiter, with his eyes on me. The wines weren't cheap so I chose the house white.

I couldn't take my eyes off his rain mac, which was at odds with our lush surroundings. I asked him if he was feeling cold. 'Not particularly,' he said, draining his cocktail and completely missing the point of my question.

I left it there.

The waiter brought the wine over. I tasted it and he poured us both a large glass. I still hadn't finished my Pimms but Mark, seemingly thirsty, took a swig straightaway.

We chatted and laughed, about all sorts of things, but remember thinking how easy it all felt. We ordered our food as Mark drained his glass and re-filled. He was going to pour more into mine, but my glass was untouched. 'Come on, drink up,' he joked. But I wondered if he'd prefer it if I didn't as he was managing to guzzle his way through the bottle. As the meal progressed, Mark began to slip little innuendos into the conversation. Something he hadn't done in any of our phone conversations, or since meeting earlier. He had that look across the eyes of a man beginning to revel in the influence of the vino he'd been guzzling. And, of course, he still had his rain mac on. It wasn't a good look.

The bill came and it was a big one. Mark waved off my offer to contribute. He laughed and said I could pay him back. It was still early and he suggested going on to a bar. It did still feel a little early to be heading home so I agreed.

Outside the restaurant Mark waved down a black cab. I climbed in first and when he joined me, he sat close. A little too close. It was the kind of personal space ignorance goaded by alcohol. It was a short journey to the place in Soho – one of those trendy, basement bars. I was thinking we'd have a drink and a chat then call it a night.

But for Mark, the night was just beginning. He asked if I wanted a drink. Having had a coffee after dinner I didn't fancy starting on the alcohol again so I said yes to an orange juice. After asking me – three times – if I wanted a 'real' drink he reluctantly ordered my juice. The bar was noisy and full of people shouting to be heard above the house music. I found us a table and Mark brought the drinks over. His first drink disappeared within minutes of sitting down so he ordered a second. He was halfway through that when his behaviour began to change.

'I'd really like to kiss you right now,' he said.

'Where did that come from?' I asked, doing my best to throw him off his sleazy comment. Besides, with the rain mac and increasingly bloodshot, roaming eyes there was no way that was going to happen.

'You look hot,' he said. He leaned towards me and I leaned back. He sat back looking sulky. 'Another drink?' he said.

'I've got one, thanks,' I motioned towards my orange juice, sitting untouched on the table.

Mark drained his glass and got up to head back towards the bar. This time, watching him walk over to the bar, he had the gait of a man trying to hide the fact he'd had one too many. He came back and sat too close – again. He said something about how sexy I looked. I said thanks and feeling uncomfortable edged away from him. He drank some more of his rum cocktail and shuffled closer. So began our dance of avoidance – me politely edging away, him shuffling nearer. Thinking back, I should have just left. I should have got up, thanked him for dinner and headed home. It's what I'd do now. But I was still a bit green and hadn't been exposed to anyone who turned sleazy after a whiff of booze. He slurped the rest of his cocktail down and went up to the bar for a third and then a fourth. By this time, his conversation had dried up. His rain mac hung loosely off his shoulders – like a snake shedding its skin. I told him I was ready to leave.

'Good idea,' he said, his eyes bloodshot but his spirits lifted. 'There's a great bar near me and the drinks are way cheaper than here. We can carry on the party there…'

Party? What party?

I declined, of course and left.

LESSON: KNOW WHEN TO LEAVE

Nervous about a date? One drink may give you the Dutch courage you need, but overdoing it never ends well. Alcohol turned Mark into a lech – complete with dodgy rain mac. Our date showed me how comfortable he was to drink alone and what his 'normal' level of alcohol consumption was. Two things that don't work for me. But it also taught me that sometimes it's perfectly acceptable to walk out. Just don't wait as long as I did.

6 The 'ghostly' one

I met Michael for lunch in Greenwich one sunny afternoon. Lunch dates are a good idea, by the way, because you're time is on a meter. Sixty minutes isn't too long to suffer if you don't like your date and it gives you a nice taster date to bounce off if you do.

Although time was short he sidled up late. He explained that he'd arrived on time but had been looking for someone shorter – I'm 5ft 6in but was wearing 3in sandals. Conversation was a little stilted at first, but we soon relaxed into a friendly chat as we headed towards a coffee shop. As soon as we stepped through the door, Michael said, 'I don't want anything."

So, it seems we weren't meeting for lunch after all. But I needed to eat something. I'd come straight from a workshop that morning and was headed to a meeting straight after our date. So I picked up a sandwich and ordered a coffee. Michael stood a comfortable distance away and I guessed it was because he didn't want there to be any confusion about who was paying. I got to the till and asked him if he was sure he wouldn't have anything. 'Ok, then," he said. 'I'll have one of these." He picked a bottle of sparkling water from the cooler and handed it to the man at the till – who promptly added it to my bill. No, I guess there was no confusion over who was paying.

Michael strode off to find a seat outside so we could enjoy the sun. I looked down at the tray and over at him through the glass, settling himself at one of the tables. I picked up the tray to follow.

Now, I wasn't expecting him to pay, especially if he wasn't

eating, and I'm not so strapped that I can't pick up the tab for a bottle of water, but not even to offer to carry the tray? So, call me old-fashioned, but I like a touch of chivalry in a man. It was obvious I wasn't going to find that here.

We chatted as I ate my sandwich and he gulped his water. We had a couple of things in common and our conversation moved around our love of different cultures and the places we'd visited. We chatted easily and I found myself papering over my shaky first impressions. Time passed quickly and it was soon time to leave. It felt as though we'd only just scratched the surface, but we both agreed that there was enough likeable ground to meet for a second date. Michael said he'd send a text to arrange something. We walked back to the station, said goodbye, kissed on the cheek and went our separate ways.

I sent him a text that evening thanking him for an interesting lunch. He responded saying we must meet again soon. So, I left him to it. Thinking he could text me when he could make the time to meet. A week later I received an almost identical text to the last one saying we must meet again soon. I sent him some dates, but I heard nothing back. After a month, I'd still not heard anything so I deleted his number. I assumed he wasn't interested and that he was most likely having difficulty telling me he wasn't interested.

I carried on dating.

Eight months passed. Then, I receive a '*Hi, hope you're well*' message from an unknown number. I replied saying I was great and asking who it was and got this reply: *You've forgotten me already. Wow. Ok let me jog your memory. It's Michael.*

In his mind, obviously, the eight-month gap between this

communication and the last might as well have been eight hours. But even better than that, he was now offended that I'd deleted his number. I asked him if he'd gotten any greyer in the time since our last conversation. He immediately sent a smiley face – his way, I'm assuming, of softening his last message and then said he'd been busy with *'this and that'*. I ended the conversation there. 'This and that' – a euphemism for *'I've been dating someone else and it hasn't worked, so I thought I'd pick back up with you'* perhaps? Whatever was going on in his life, I'd lost interest, say, about seven months earlier after waiting for him to confirm our second date. And with no explanation for his sudden disappearance, or an apology for leaving me hanging, I really didn't see the need to go on.

LESSON: GHOSTING ISN'T ABOUT YOU

*When someone ghosts you the easy 'go-to' place is to wonder what **you** might have done, or said, wrong. But realise this: it's never about you. People who ghost are mostly either rude or cowards.*
Dating is meant to be fun. You're supposed to communicate with, and meet, lots of people. So everyone should be open about the fact they're going on other dates. If you're interested in someone else or didn't enjoy the date just say so - and if you can't face a phone call do it in a text.
If you're on the receiving end, accept that you'll probably never know why they've stopped calling. They've either met someone else: coward. Or they think it's best to act as though you never existed: rude. Either way, don't take it personally.

7 The 'almost compatible' one

Wayne was a vibrant, playful, creative man who'd emigrated to Canada aged seven. He'd been back in England for a couple of years and had only recently signed up to the site where we met. We were the same age and shared similar cultural references. Our messages quickly developed into phone conversations – both mediums were interesting and easy, and we talked about everything from music and culture to politics and stupid stuff. We clicked from the very first message in my inbox. What happened was my fault really as, in the excitement of our refreshing conversations, I forgot to check his profile for my non-negotiables.

Our date was in central London. We met at the Nike store at Oxford Circus. He was late. Later than me. He wasn't what I'd expected – small with a lean build. He hadn't lied about how he looked, he just seemed different in the flesh somehow. He wore cargo pants, a checked shirt and an oversized knitted cap. He looked a little crumpled, but when he smiled it reached his whole face. We found a coffee shop nearby and had lots to talk about. He looked nervous at first – something about the way he sat, leaning forward with clasped hands. But he was very open, sharing a lot about his childhood, becoming a father too young and his regrets about not physically having had the chance to live with his son.

We moved onto a second, more intimate café and it was here that our non-negotiables came up. Number one on his list was he wanted children. Number one on my list was I didn't. Having not been around for his son he wanted the 'children-with-a-house-in-the-suburbs' ideal. He wanted to experience living with his children as he watched them grow up, comfort them at night as they teethed, take them to school, go on family holidays. He wanted all the things he'd missed as a young dad who'd been absent through circumstance. Even five years ago, he'd have been perfect for me. I loved that he wanted to be a family man. But one thing men don't have to consider is what it's like to carry a baby. Or that getting pregnant actually isn't that easy or even necessarily a given – especially with an approaching-50-pre-menopausal-body.

It was a point neither of us could see any way past. And for the first time on our date we fell silent. It was a harsh reminder of my own waning fertility. And that men my age could still want the very thing I'd reluctantly conceded – as a late forty-something woman with a grown child – was behind me.

Our date ended on a bittersweet vibe. Wayne was keen for us to stay in touch. He'd made lots of friends dating online and saw this as another chance to do the same. It seemed like a good idea – a good way to enjoy each other's company without all the relationship stuff. I wasn't so sure but agreed to try.

We kept in contact by phone and text every few days, filling each other in on the day we'd had or plans for the weekend. It was cool. We agreed to meet up a second time and that's where it was clear that this 'friends' thing was going to be hard to maintain. You've met and connected because you're attracted to each other. You're on the site because you're looking for a partner, not a friend. You have to ask yourself how you'd feel if your new 'friend' found himself the perfect girlfriend. The one who could give him the children he craved. The reality is you'll feel like crap. You'll be reminded of your shortcomings and will have to smile and say all the things you'd prefer not to. Don't do it. Be kind to yourself.

We agreed to meet up on a couple of occasions and I bailed on him. There was a battle going on inside and the rational part of me was losing. So, after a few weeks of regular contact, I reluctantly let go.

LESSON: BE REALISTIC ABOUT THE FRIEND ZONE

Honestly? I was a coward. What I'm going to tell you to do, and what I should have done, is be upfront. Tell him straight that you don't think staying in touch is such a good idea.

I should have wished him well, then slipped away, but some deluded part of me was thinking that if I continued, everything would work itself out. It's that feeling you get when you're compatible with a person. When you enjoy their company, vibe on the same level, love being in their space and think, I've found someone! But the reality in my case was that the thing he wanted wasn't going to change and neither was I. Staying friends can be hard to maintain when you're so compatible, so don't try.

8 The 'lecherous' one

I didn't recognise Byron at first. Not from his profile pic or his ad. We'd worked together some years back. We weren't colleagues per se but worked for the same organisation in different departments and had mutual friends through work. I knew of him but didn't know him. I soon learned he was an engineer and a few years younger than me.

Over the next couple of weeks we communicated by phone and text. He talked a lot about his upbringing. About the love he had for his grandmother who'd raised him alone when his mother had left. He'd spent a lot of time around women growing up and had a healthy respect for them, he said. He was complimentary without being sleazy and sent cute texts just because.

Our date was in a country pub and because we'd previously worked together and got on so well, I did something I usually don't. I agreed to let him pick me up. It wasn't the best move in my dating history. Getting into his car was like flicking his testosterone switch to overdrive. On the way to the pub if he could have pressed the accelerator through the floor he would have. My right foot hurt from pressing the floor in a desperate search for a brake. I asked him if he was in a rush. If the restaurant was about to close. If he would… Just. Slow. DOWN!!

He eased up then and laughed. 'Sorry," he said. 'I love speed. But I'm guessing you like it slow." It was such a cheesy line I had to laugh. Out loud. It wasn't the kind of thing you could take seriously. I mean, who says that sort of stuff? It's the kind of line you'd only find in a badly written romantic novel. He looked at me, blinked, but said nothing.

We arrived at the pub not long afterwards. It was in a secluded spot, surrounded by green – cherry trees, bushes, grass, and little else. There were no other buildings and, apart from an old lady at a bus stop up the road there were hardly any people either.

As soon as we stepped out of the car, his whole persona changed. He insisted on walking behind me and commenting on my 'curves", my 'sexy walk", my bum. And all before we'd reached the pub entrance. I wasn't worried as much as I was surprised. We've all met guys that think this is *the* way to compliment a woman, but until now he hadn't seemed like that type. If he wasn't wearing the same face, I'd be convinced he was a different person.

Inside, a few people – mainly couples – were scattered around. A waitress seated us in a booth and as I sat down, he said he needed to use the loo. While he was gone I browsed the menu, scanned the room and checked my phone. All the things you do when you want to avoid looking uncomfortable.

He came back and we ordered food and, on his insistence, a bottle of expensive wine. We chatted about the usual stuff – work, dating, life. I asked him to tell me more about his background and it seemed he'd forgotten his own back story. A Cuban father became South African and when I challenged him on it he said I'd obviously misheard him. Then, with a forkful of vegetable lasagne halfway to my mouth, he leaned forward – with a look I think he was hoping would come across sensuous, but which actually looked a little pained – and asked what my favourite sexual position was. He spoke just like he was asking me my favourite colour or dress or holiday destination. I have to thank him on his timing – I would have choked otherwise. I opened my mouth to say something and he jumped in first, 'Sorry, I need the loo again." And off he went.

I wondered if he had bladder problems.

'Everything okay?" I said when he came back.

He nodded, stretched out his hand to stroke my arm. I reached for my wine.

'So, that's a full on question for a first date."

He smiled, leant back in his chair and started eating again. 'Not on first dates with me." He had a serious case of Cheddar.

It was a good time to change the subject so I asked about his childhood. It was his opportunity to tell me that it was where his love of older women had developed. It was one of those households that people naturally gravitate to. As the only boy in the house he often found himself in the company of his mum and grandmum's friends. As he went through puberty it was also when he had his first sexual encounter – with an older woman who visited the house.

Ewww… TMI Alert!

'That's why I prefer older women," he said. 'You know yourselves. Know what you want. You're more sexy…" This said with the same pained expression he'd shown me earlier.

Ok, so now I was ready for this date to end, but as we'd travelled over together, there wasn't going to be an easy exit strategy.

The waitress was at the next table and when I caught her eye I silently gestured that we were ready for the bill.

'I should be getting back now," I said.

Byron looked disappointed, but nodded. 'I just need to…"

and he motioned towards the loo again.

He had to have some sort of bladder condition. Or maybe he was nervous on some level and it was manifesting itself through his bowel. We'd been here little over an hour and this was his third time. I knew I couldn't let it pass. When he eventually returned to the table I said: 'I'm sorry, but I've got to ask, have you got a bladder problem?"

His response summed him up.

'No, babe," he said. 'You're so hot, I keep having to w***."

I caught a taxi home.

LESSON: EVEN WORKMATES CAN BE STRANGERS

I made a huge mistake with Byron. I allowed him to take me somwhere quite secluded in his car. I dropped my guard because we'd worked in the same place, but even people you work with can still be strangers. However comfortable you think you feel, make your own way to your dates. As soon as I stepped in to his car I gave up my control and personal safety. I was at his mercy. Get to know your date before you let them take you anywhere.

9 The 'narcissitic' one

I noticed his smile first. Wide, white and wonderful. I was waiting outside the tube station and saw a tall, lean man jog casually across the road towards me. With a flat cap, short rain mac and a man bag slung across him this guy looked cool. If my date looks this good I thought I'll be happy. He looked at me then and smiled, showing a mouth packed with teeth. It took only a second to realise that he *was* my date.

First impressions count. That's what you always hear. But what first impressions? The first time you see them? Hear their voice? Hear them snore? With Ray my first impression was about his energy. His vibe. He had a cool way about him. He seemed calm. At ease with himself.

He suggested a pub that sat in the shadow of the London Eye. He got the drinks in, while I found us a table. Apart from a few people having post-work drinks the pub was surprisingly quiet for it's location. But then, it was a Monday night. Ray came over with the drinks, took his mac and cap off then settled into the curved corner seat I'd found. We sipped big drinks and made small talk. It was our ice-breaker, our way in to the interesting stuff, the proper stuff. Then Ray brought the conversation around to his work as a healer. He talked about his previous existence working in marketing, about a spiritual awakening he'd had, about his love of essential oils and their properties, about his travels, about the people he'd met. He told me about the months of migraines he'd suffered before having a spiritual experience that changed his life, about the problems this caused with his girlfriend at the time. And for the next hour Ray talked about his life, his challenges, his healing business, his work, his holiday… He stopped only to let me ask questions. About him. Halfway through, feeling bored and redundant I decided to see how long it would take him to ask me something. But Ray was on a roll and I really didn't want to stop his flow since this had become something of an experiment. We were there for another half hour before Ray asked me something. 'Are you hungry?" he said. 'I'm hungry. Let's go eat."

Listening to him talk had made me hungry so I decided to go with it. Sometimes on dates you have to make a judgement call. Maybe he was nervous and didn't realise he was rambling on. But more importantly, there were the text messages leading up to the date. In those he'd seemed genuinely interested in my thoughts, in the things I had to say. He asked questions, he engaged. The man sitting opposite me wasn't what I'd been expecting.

We left the pub in search of something more satisfying to eat. When we found a restaurant we liked the look of, I decided to take control of the date. We browsed the menu, ordered our food and then I said, 'Let's take turns to ask each other questions about each other." You can guess my thinking. If he wasn't going to ask me anything off his own back, maybe he could be encouraged to if we turned it into a game.

'Why don't you go first," I said.

'Ok." He smiled his wide, white smile. 'When you first saw me crossing the road did you fancy me?"

It took all my self-control not to throttle him. So, even when being coaxed into asking me about me, it was, yet again, all about him. I asked if he had another question he'd like to ask about me. 'Yes," he said. 'Can I kiss you?"

So there it was. He wasn't interested in me at all. It was more about what I thought about him. When our date ended I decided that would be the end of it. But then his texts continued and in those he was the ebullient, attentive and enquiring man that had convinced me to go on our first date. We agreed to meet again. And again. Each time we had a better time than the last. He got better at two-way conversation, but still something gnawed at my gut. On our fourth date, when I asked him to tell me about his life before the spiritual experience he talked about constantly, he said: 'If we're going to get on, it'll be better if you just don't ask me anything about my life before."

I only needed to be told once. We didn't see each other again.

LESSON: TRUST YOUR GUT

Nature has blessed us with this in-built sixth sense to help us cut through the bullshit. But we don't always use it. How often have you had that bad feeling in the pit of your stomach that something isn't quite right? Usually, it's because something isn't. Sometimes, we're so convinced someone is right for us that we bury that feeling deep in our bellies. We're scared that if we walk away, we'll end up sad and alone. But regardless of how we pretend it isn't there, that feeling will come up again. Ray made it easy for me. He confirmed in one sentence that my initial instinct was right. First impressions do count. Always listen to your gut.

10 The 'I'm a catfish' one

I was just home from work when my phone beeped with a new message. His profile intrigued me. We loved some of the same books, we had similar interests and he was eloquent and funny. He had just one profile picture – a head and shoulder shot revealing a man possibly in his early thirties. He had a full head of black hair neatly cropped into short, back and sides with a perfect five o'clock shadow. He wore glasses and a smile that gave his face a kind look. I had to respond. He came back instantly with lots of questions. He seemed genuinely interested in what I had to say. I asked him why just the one picture and he explained that a) he had very few of himself and b) this was the best one. I thought no more about it. We exchanged phone numbers and over the next two weeks kept in regular contact. He was a deeply spiritual man and we spent lots of time reflecting on life and where we both wanted to be. It was around this time that his picture and profile disappeared from the site. It felt a bit early to be deleting profiles, but I guess I felt flattered that he felt he'd found someone that showed enough potential to warrant deleting his profile. Our text conversations became quite profound – I felt as if I was getting to know this man on a much deeper level. At this point, I hadn't met a suitable man in weeks. I'd begun to feel disillusioned and ready to jack it all in. But it always seems that just when you're about to give up, some new opportunity presents itself. This connection was just that.

It wasn't long before our first phone conversation. His voice was deep and mellifluous – listening to him speak was easy. He had three children, but lived on his own. After numerous messages and texts and a number of phone calls he still hadn't suggested meeting, so I did.

His reply: 'Yes, we must meet soon.'

'Well, why don't we fix a time now' I said.

'Um…' he said. He continued, 'I'm really looking forward to meeting you, but I'm being headhunted by two companies at the moment so really need to focus on the work I'm being asked to prepare for both jobs. Can we meet once that's all over?'

It seemed feasible. Yes, there was a distant alarm going off in my head, but I had no idea why. So, I told him to contact me when he wasn't so busy, then signed off leaving the ball in his court.

I put him out of my mind and got on with life. I chatted to other people through the website, but no one really caught my attention the way he had. Somewhere within, I was holding out for a meeting, but I didn't want to push it. I focused on work and simply carried on.

Six weeks later, I got a text message from him. It said simply: 'Hey stranger.' We chatted about everything that had happened since the last time we spoke. I broached the subject of meeting again and he agreed. I asked him to send me another picture. It wasn't a test. I really did want to be reminded of what he looked like. He laughed and said at 6ft 4in I wouldn't be able to miss him as he'd probably be the tallest person in the room. I laughed too, happy that we were finally going to meet. We agreed on a bar halfway between our homes. I arrived with a couple of minutes to spare. I ordered some tea and took a seat at a table opposite the door. I phoned him to let him know I'd arrived to which he replied that he was just pulling up outside.

I felt nervous in my stomach. We got on so well on the phone. We had stuff in common. I liked the way he looked in his picture. I decided not to look at the door, to let him maintain the mystery until we were face to face. So when he approached the table I didn't see him. I heard his voice first: those deep, rich tones now so recognizable. I looked up. But the man in front of me wasn't the man in his picture. This man with the familiar, sonorous tone reminded me of Gandalf. Ok, so his beard wasn't quite so white or quite so long. But to my point: he looked NOTHING like his picture. Through magic or makeover he had transformed into a different person.

His picture: black hair, cropped at the sides and spiky on top.
His reality: a bald crown with white hair at the sides and back.

His picture: a chiseled, youthful face
His reality: a generously rounded face with a double chin

His picture: a head shot
His reality: a portly middle-aged spread

He was nervous and we both knew why. I was disappointed that someone I really got on with had actually begun our liaison with a lie. He ordered tea and sat down and the date began. I went through the motions, not really knowing how I'd bring up the whole 'photo' topic. So we talked about everything else besides – his new job, my work, the hotel bar, the tea… and through it all I imagined him in a pointed wizard hat, brandishing a wand.

Eventually, I explained that I needed the loo, made my excuses and darted off to the little girl's room. I needed to reassess the situation. I leaned on the sink and stared at myself in the mirror. 'You have to say something,' I urged myself. 'You can't let him get away with this.' I took a deep breath. My reflection was right.

I went back to the table. He smiled. It was the first time in the hour we'd spent chatting that he looked genuinely relaxed and I realised it was probably because rather than dart out of the nearest exit, I'd returned to our table.

I inhaled, deeply. 'You've been a bit naughty, haven't you,.

'Naughty,' He said. 'How so?'

'Well, you don't look anything like your picture,' I said.

'There's a reason for that,' he said, shifting in his seat. Here's what he said:

I was on holiday some years back when I was in a life-threatening accident. The driver of the car I was in was killed and I woke up in hospital four weeks later with no recollection of the accident or anything since. I'm told I was in a coma. My daughters were flown out because the doctors weren't sure I'd survive. It was touch and go. My life took a massive turn.

When I woke up I faced months of physiotherapy. A couple of my teeth had been knocked out in the accident and a few more were damaged. Over the time I was in hospital my hair went grey – quickly. And I gained weight.

It was a horrible story, and I told him how sorry I was to hear it. But, despite this, the small voice in my head was wondering what this had to do with his totally inaccurate profile picture. So, I stayed silent. I'll give him the space to fully explain I thought. There'll be a perfect explanation for why he posted a picture on his profile that bore no resemblance to who he was now. I just had to give him time to get to the end.

I realised that while I'd been lost in my own thoughts he'd stopped speaking. I wondered if I'd missed the end. Then he said, 'So, what I'm trying to say is that picture is of me just before the accident. It's how I like to remember myself.'

It was a poignant story and I felt for him. But it still didn't account for why he'd used such an old picture of himself. A picture so different I was convinced it was another person.

We'd finished our tea by this point and although he asked if I wanted more, it felt like an empty gesture. There wasn't anything more to say. His deception had killed the date.

LESSON: NEVER LIE ABOUT WHO YOU ARE

People lie for many reasons online: feelings of insecurity; to boost their confidence; to make you fall for them before you meet... The problem is you can only maintain the lies for as long as it takes to meet in person. At this point there's no hiding. When we're building relationships, an important part of that is physical attraction. It's why profile pictures are so important and why lying about your appearance transcends all other dating faux pas. I've yet to meet anyone who could get past it.

Step Four

Mate

13

Sex talk

Like so many words in the English language 'mate' has its share of meanings. It can be defined as a friend, a life partner, or simply just a lover. And it's these three definitions we're going to explore here. Sex will come up (pardon the pun) fairly early on in our liaisons, so let's start there. And, especially for the ladies over 60, the news is good. According to a recent Match.com study women are having the best sex of their lives at age 66. Apparently, men aren't far behind, with an average of 63. Maybe it's because we know what we want by then. We also know what we like and, more importantly, no longer care what anyone thinks. Whatever the reason our modern SEXagenarians are living up to their name.

But what about first date sex? It's still one of those questions no one quite knows how to answer. It was bad enough when we were scrabbling about as teens. Now, we've been through the relationship mill (maybe once, maybe twice, possibly countless times) and we all still want to know what's acceptable or how we'll be perceived if we 'go there' on a first date.

Society still touts a different answer depending on the gender of the person involved. It's interesting that in many cases, despite 21st Century sexual liberalism, these old-fashioned perceptions haven't changed that much: if a man sleeps around he's a stud; if a woman does she's a slut.

We think we're sexually freer than we used to be. But are we really? So often nowadays, sexual freedom is defined by how quickly we're prepared to say yes, rather than actually having the choice to say yes *or* no. Take the three-date rule for example, which says sex after date three is the norm. But who decided this? Shouldn't we feel empowered to decide whether sex on date one, three, five or seven is right for us and *not* be judged either way for it?

When talking to a male friend of mine recently he told me that when men are looking at profile pictures of women, they're already thinking about having sex with them. Everything else will hopefully just get them to that point. If that's true, then no one should be judge or jury. First date sex doesn't mean you can't go on to develop a long-term relationship. Nor does it have to mean sexual promiscuity – especially not on the part of the woman. Sometimes people just want to have sex. Who should care what gender they are? So if not the first date, then when? Whenever feels right for you is the obvious answer. But Cheryl McClary, professor of Women's Health at the University of North Carolina-Asheville has it spot on. She says men should: "Make sure their brain, heart and penis are in a straight line before they have sex". It can't hurt for women to do the same (minus the penis, of course!).

Sarah, an ex-colleague signed up to an online dating site a few years ago. She was active online, managing to arrange at least two or three dates a week. The build up was always the same. She'd exchange a few texts with her date and arrange to meet within a few days of first communicating. She almost always dated on work nights and almost always drank too much during the date. The next morning she'd come to work in the same clothes and share all about the night's events. She slept with the majority of her first dates. The point was she didn't see sex on the first date as a problem. She wanted to see how she clicked with them. She saw first date sex as a necessity. She didn't want to start dating someone and find a few months in that the sex was bad.

I, on the other hand, have never had sex on a first date. Not because I'm against it, or because I'm judging anyone who does. I just haven't felt that kind of instant and overwhelming connection I'd need to allow that to happen. But if you do, go for it. Some women worry that the person they've had sex with on the first date will lose respect for them. But it takes two. You both did it. Which makes no one person better or worse than the other, whatever society wants to encourage you to believe.

Nowadays, many long-term relationships have been sparked by first date sex. It's also been shown that sex on the first date can mean different things to different people. It's just as immature to assume every woman who has sex on the first date is promiscuous, as it is to believe that every man with size 12 feet is well hung.

Still a taboo?

We're more exposed to sex and eroticism than ever before, but we're still not talking about it. Not really. The problem is over-exposure. We're bombarded by images, by videos, by news stories. After a while you just, kinda, switch off. And there's a whole generation of people living vicariously through the tangled relationship webs of celebrities, or worse – internet porn. People are basing their beliefs about 'normal' sex on what they see on the internet.

It seems that most people looking for serious relationships (that's women *and* men) would prefer to wait. We'd prefer to get to know each other. Spend time with each other without getting physical.

HOW LONG PEOPLE WILL WAIT TO HAVE SEX

- 18% would sleep with someone on the first date
- 12% follow the three-date rule
- 15% wait to fall in love first
- 5% would wait until they're married

And 1 in 3 women over 55 wouldn't sleep with a partner until they're in love

*YouGov survey, February 2017

It stands to reason. Getting physical with someone very early on means you don't know each other. You're both still showing your best side, trying to convince each other you're the perfect match. But the flip side of this is anxiety. Sleep with someone you don't want to see again and you could end up worrying how to get out of seeing him again. Sleep with someone you like and you'll worry what he might think of you. Think about it too much beforehand and you'll probably abstain. Anxiety is a passion killer.

However, if you *are* online just for sex, download the apps that are specifically geared towards people looking for casual hook ups. Don't waste time on the more general sites where the majority of people are looking for something more serious.

Sexually transmitted diseases

You're re-entering the dating world often after decades in a long-term relationship. It's a landscape that's changed but often your behaviours haven't. You've had the same partner for as long as you can remember. In some cases, maybe your only partner. And because you've been together for so long and may even be menopausal, you've grown used to not using protection.

But because so many 45-64 year-olds have taken these attitudes into the dating world the incidences of sexually transmitted diseases (STIs) in this group have rocketed.

In a younger generation that have lived through the aftermath of the AIDS crisis there's no real stigma attached to getting yourself checked for STIs. But ask your average 50+ man or woman when they last saw the inside of a Genitourinary (GUM) clinic and quite often the answer is silence. Sex is an inevitable part of dating, and, as a consequence, if you're not practicing safe sex so are STIs, so:

- **Always use a condom.** The menopause will stop you getting pregnant, but it won't prevent you from contracting chlamydia, gonorrhea, syphilis, gential warts, herpes, AIDS etc etc.
- **You're only recognised as being in the menopause** when you haven't had a period for 12 consecutive months. Anything less than that and you can still get pregnant.
- **Have yourself regularly tested for STIs** if you're sleeping with different partners
- **Ask your sexual partners** when they were last tested.
- **Get a self-test kit** you can use at home if you prefer not to visit a GUM clinic
- **Insist you and your new partner are tested** before starting any new relationship.

14

Are we there yet?

Growing up the only girl in a family of many boys it's really no surprise that I grew up a tomboy. Our road was brimming with baby boomers and with so many kids around and a six-pack of brothers I had lots of Boy. Friends.

I was comfortable in male company. The boys that were always at our house were just brothers without the same blood. They were my brother's friends and they were my mates. I didn't have to make an effort. Of course, that was before my hormone-fuelled teens and those first tentative steps towards self-awareness. As the first moody signs of puberty began to emerge, so did the realisation that these mates of my brothers were also often attractive members of the opposite sex.

Enter Leyton: my brother's friend and first crush. He was gorgeous. I wasn't the only one who thought it and, of course, he had no shortage of beautiful girls willing to be his striking other half. He had that universal attractiveness. The kind that most people would agree put him in a category a little above the rest of us. I found myself tongue-tied when he was around. And I wished I had even the faintest hint of style about me. I began to make more of an effort with myself if I knew he was coming round. I'd pull a skirt out from my measly wardrobe. Make a failed attempt at re-plaiting my cornrows or patting down my messy afro. I never had the bottle to actually tell him how I felt and he never once treated me any differently – even though I'm sure he must have guessed. We continued on as friends and after a time it did just wear off, but on reflection it did make me think about that word: mate. And how when you're in a relationship the aim is to have both definitions of the word: a friend and a long-term partner.

I met Warren – a personal trainer – on dating app Tindr. I'd swiped left so often before he appeared on my phone that I was about to give up. He had penned thoughtful lines about himself when I clicked through to his profile. I swiped right and my phone whirred. We were a match. All the usual messages, texts and phone calls followed over the next few weeks and we decided to meet.

We went to a plush hotel bar for afternoon cocktails. He was good company, and we spent the whole afternoon together before agreeing to meet for lunch a couple of days later. That date went well and we had four more dates in quick succession. He was a friend as well as someone I was 'seeing'. The best combination. We were enjoying each other's company, had shared the fact we were both looking for someone long-term and wanted to continue to see each other. But admitting it also came with certain assumptions. That we were going to be exclusive, that we'd stop looking.

When you reach this stage in the dating process, it's natural to make such assumptions. These days, most of us know at least one couple that has met online. And if you don't you certainly know someone that's at least tried it. People speak openly about the dates they've gone on; the experiences they've had; the new partners they've started relationships with; the husbands and wives they've found. We've heard how these relationships develop after those first few dates, once the couples have decided to commit and we assume it's going to be the same for us.

But even when you've reached this stage, people have different ideas about how to proceed. I discovered this with Warren when I decided to bring the subject up during one of our conversations.

When to have 'the conversation'

So, you've had date four, five, six. Things are going well. Date seven rolls around, followed by eight and nine. But, 10? No, no. NO. When you're approaching double figures, 'date' no longer sounds appropriate. Tell your friends you're going on your tenth or eleventh and they'll wonder why you haven't talked about whether you've arrived at 'destination: relationship'.

By now, you know more about each other. You're becoming

used to each other's idiosyncracies. You've both decided you like each other enough to want to spend regular time together. But no one has broached the topic. Why have things not progressed? Is there a reason the two of you are still 'dating'?

Warren and I hadn't actually discussed how we'd move forward. We'd talked generally about what we wanted when we first met, and then went on to enjoy date after delicious date. I'd convinced myself that this was the start of something, but neither of us had actually confirmed it.

After a few more great dates, I decided to raise the subject during a phone call. I needed reassurance that he was in the same place as me; that he was feeling as if we had something we were *both* happy to develop. Despite the fact we'd agreed we were looking for the same thing, we hadn't talked about whether we'd found it with each other. It turns out that although Warren had enjoyed our dates, he wanted to continue to see me *and* other people.

I'd made certain assumptions and they were wrong. But assumptions aren't fact. The only way to know for sure is to ask. Conversations that matter are never easy to initiate; especially when it's about your future with someone. We're scared to broach the subject in case they don't feel quite the same. So what do we do instead? We try to make up our own mind about how our 'partner' might be feeling. We check the app to see if they're still active, and are upset if we find they're online. We forget, though, that they could be having the same doubts and insecurities as we are. Instead we let paranoia fuel our actions. And paranoia is one of the most destructive forces in early relationships.

If you find yourself in this place, the conversation about whether or not to start a relationship is overdue. Take a deep breath, then ask.

15

Making it work

Men. Women. We're different: Mars and Venus and all that. But what does it actually mean for our relationships. We've already seen how psychologists studying gender differences in methods of communication have revealed the more direct and practical way men express themselves and the more feeling-centred way that women do.

So, we can accept that men and women may have different approaches; that each gender expects and needs different things from a partner. Understanding this and putting it into practice isn't always that easy. The beautiful thing about a relationship that started online is how and why you connected. You've eliminated the uncertainty there can be around initial attraction. You know they're single. You know they like you too. You've cut to the chase and established a connection you're both clear about. But no one teaches us what it takes to maintain a relationship once we've established we want to be together.

As humans, we're good at complicating things. It's the reason there are thousands of books out there on this subject, all with different ideas about what it takes to make a relationship work. Over time, I've simmered it down to two things.

The first is recognising that we're all still children. Agreed, we're housed in adult bodies, but do we ever really grow up inside? And it's due to the lack of actual life lessons we receive. Think about it, we're taught how to recite the times tables by rote; how the body works; about great works of literature or key scientific discoveries. But where's the schooling in how to find compromise in a relationship, to apologise when you're wrong or in dealing with infidelity or abusive behaviour. So, like anything we lack schooling in, we remain eternal children, looking for lessons where we can find them. Our childhoods aren't called our formative years without good reason.

The second is amnesia. Soon after we start a relationship, it begins to set in. We're usually unaware of it, and the rate at which it develops varies from person to person. But, like some of the more debilitating forms of memory loss, relationship amnesia is a condition that also comes on slowly. Over time we forget what attracted us to our partner in the first place, we forget the things we did when we first dated, we forget the memories we've made, we forget why we were happy; we forget how to just be friends.

So, with these two things in mind, I've put together the top 10 ways to nurture the relationship with your new partner. They're suggestions from over 200 men and women I've spoken to about what makes and keeps them happy in a relationship and from my own experiences. Think of these 10 things as the compass to help you navigate your way through your relationship.

1 Be life daters

Remember the fun you had when you were first dating? The anticipation you felt at the thought of seeing that person again. You may have tried new or interesting things or just spent time getting to know each other. Then when ordinary life kicks in, we forget to put aside time to spend together just because.

Overcome this by agreeing to be life daters. Make space for time as a couple by allocating regular date nights, to remember how you felt back then. Don't let everyday routine leech the energy out of your relationship.

2 Feed your inner 'child'

Allocate time to try new things. When we learn new things we're like children again. Do these things together and you'll laugh together, be silly together, and embrace being vulnerable together. When we learn new things it also encourages us to ask questions. We learn even more about each other and ourselves. Part of the excitement of a new relationship is discovering who this person is over time. It's a mini adventure and a chance to play.

As boys men are taught to play in a very different way to girls. Boys are encouraged to be active. To take part in activities where they can assert their masculinity. Girls are taught to be nurturers and our play involves being carers and caring. All, supposedly, to shape our roles in society. But play is as important in a relationship as it is when we're young. Playing together provides the opportunity to create happy memories, to reinforce the reasons you're together. Giving yourselves the time to be children will keep the energy of your relationship alive.

3 Don't sweat the small stuff

Niggly stuff. There's always something about your partner that annoys you. It's normal. But there are ways to deal with this stuff. It's healthy to create the kind of relationship where you can talk. But know how to do it. The worst way to start any conversation is by criticising someone because no one responds well to criticism or blame. Be emotionally intelligent. Your partner is checking out the way you deal with every situation. Will you become over emotional or irrational? Will you use logic? At the start of a relationship, the way we deal with a crisis can be the make or break of it.

We already know that we're prone to emotional outbursts. So, don't blame them for something going wrong. Instead be practical. Appeal to their logic. Don't ignore the little things that niggle you and don't freak out when they bring stuff about you to the table.

But this process will take the two of you. You both need to be prepared to communicate. If one is reluctant or refuses, you'll never resolve anything and your relationship will suffer.

4 Get clued up

Something you can both do is watch out for the clues your partner gives about the things they like or dislike. When you see something take notice and remember it. It could be as simple as leaving your toiletries all over the place or leaving smelly socks on the floor. If you're going to live together acknowledging these things will help. It's the minor stuff that becomes major stuff over time. They may even be areas you'll have to compromise on at some point.

5 Be flirts

We see flirting as a process we use to get someone, not as something we can use to keep the spirit of our relationship alive. But it works because it's playful and can be the prelude to great sex. Text-flirt with suggestive messages throughout the day, and on date nights imagine you're on your first date again. How did you flirt then? Whether you're making eye contact or touching playfully flirt like you're single again.

6 Feel body confident

Forget all the images of 50+ celebrities with near-perfect butts, gravity-defying boobs and flawless, airbrushed skin. If you had a personal trainer, stylist, nutritionist and cook you'd look the same. These ads only serve to make us feel more insecure about how we look. You've got him. He fancies you. All you've got to do now is fancy yourself.

As women we're way too critical of ourselves. According to research conducted at the Dermatology Division of UCLA Medical Center in Los Angeles 85-98% of post pubertal women have cellulite, but look in the thousands of airbrushed images worldwide and we all feel like we're the exception. Nothing turns a man off so much as a woman who's unhappy with her body. Even moreso because quite often he loves your body just as it is.

So be proud of your bod. And if you're not do something about it. Buy yourself some sexy underwear – or take your partner out shopping and get them to buy you some. And wear it. Don't leave it folded away in your chest of drawers for a special day. Make each day special, whatever your outerwear. Wearing sexy underwear helps you feel sexy.

7 Laugh often

I love men who can make me laugh. Laughter is good for the spirit. It's also a muscle relaxant because it expands your blood vessels increasing the flow of your blood to all areas of the body. People who laugh a lot are less stressed – it decreases the release of the stress hormone apparently – which makes for less intra-relationship tension. There's also something special about understanding someone's humour and knowing how to tap into it to extract a satisfying belly laugh. It not only releases endorphins, our happy hormones, but it brings you closer together.

8 Be powerful

There is nothing more appealing, or sexy, to a man than a powerful woman, but we can sometimes confuse this idea of power with physical things such as financial or employment successes. No. Personal power is something that is generated inside. It's a belief in yourself and your abilities, whatever you choose to do in life.

It's about recognising your imperfections and embracing them. It's about having the confidence to see the mistakes you make as opportunities to learn rather than reasons to fail. It also means you don't take yourself or situations too seriously.

Don't confuse being powerful with not wanting or needing a man. Men want to feel that they're needed, so it's about establishing each of your roles in a relationship. These roles will depend entirely on how you both interact. What might work for one couple, may be wrong for the next so avoid comparing yourselves to your friends' relationships. You're aiming to be two powerful individuals, nurturing a relationship that's right for you.

9 Make room for each other

Try something your partner likes. And get them to do the same. Have a go at golf, go on a spa day, watch a romcom or the footie. You don't have to become an aficionado just give it a go and have fun in the sharing. Introduce playful competitive banter in the run up to the activity. Pretend you were a school champion even if you weren't. Winning or losing is irrelevant, but you'll share a playfulness around something your paretner is interested in.

Two of my male friends, both in contented, happy relationships, told me that over the years they've always made the effort to find out what women want. One, admitted reading all sorts of articles in women's magazines, watched romcoms, read the odd Mills & Boon. He made the point that as women we assume that men know what we want and how. But it's most often not the case.

As women we've grown up in this regime of puffed up romanticism. As pre-teen girls we'd read the girlie magazines aimed at early teens. As early teens we'd read the magazines aimed at late teens. We were never happy the age we were. We wanted to experience all the things that older girls did so we could feel more mature. We talk about it with our girlfriends. We expect men to act in a certain way. We want them to send us flowers at work so all our colleagues can coo over how lucky we are, or book a romantic weekend away just because. As much as we might deny it we want our guy to measure up way higher than our friends' boyfriends.

But guys haven't grown up doing these things, so we can't assume they'll know this stuff. They've grown up nurturing the inner adrenalin junky, reading car magazines or fawning over lad's mags. So, while we're looking for them to show off their romantic side, they're secretly hoping for a woman who'll jump out of a plane with them.

So, we all have to do a little more to reach the same page. I'm surrounded by couples that have figured that out: singles who've found the perfect person for them and have turned their meeting into great relationships. Of course, it helps that they've all been in a number of relationships prior to the one they're in now. It's clear they've learnt from those experiences. But what works in each of these relationships is how much they each extend themselves to make the other person feel comfortable.

10 Balance your lives

Remember that before you were a couple you were individuals. If you have children you also made time to be a parent. So, already we've established two possible areas of your life that you've been nurturing prior to entering this relationship. It's common to spend more time with a new partner when you're first starting out but maintaining a relationship is all about balance. Finding a point that allows you to nurture the two/three areas of your life so they are in harmony.

Once you're past the honeymoon period you need to give equal time to the different parts of your life. Spend time together as a couple, time as a family or step-family if either of you have children, and have time to do stuff on your own.

If there's an exercise class or a hobby you've always enjoyed, continue to enjoy it. And don't drop your friends. Those relationships need even more nurturing now you're with someone – both so your partner can get to know your friends and so they don't feel they've lost you.

And have fun, always

This book is meant to help you enjoy dating. From setting up your profile to emails, texts and instant messaging. From phone conversations to Skype calls. From first dates to perfect mates you are ready to take control of your dating experiences.

Take your time through each step and let your dates reveal themselves. Be open to meeting as many people as you can – you'll learn more about yourself in the process. You'll also benefit from introductions to people with the same values, morals and interests as you. And you'll know all the pitfalls from the word go.

Enjoy the process. Each level is a way to learn more about your date, so don't rush it. And have fun. Be honest about how you feel and what you're looking for. Be flexible about the qualities you need in a partner and stand firm about your non-negotiables. But most of all be patient. Finding someone can take time.

I dated online for over two years before I found a man I truly connected with (read the first part of our story over the page) and from his first message to the start of our relationship we followed this method. Which means I've joined the ranks of successful online daters. Now, three years later it's also led to an exciting new chapter in my life following my relocation to France.

If I can find success through online dating, you can too.

epilogue

The Parisian

His first message was short. *You have a beautiful smile.* Two pictures were attached. The first was taken from a distance; he was sitting in a wrought iron chair, the back of which was pushed up against a table – like the ones you find on the continent, sprawled outside restaurants and populated with smokers, people watchers and lazy lunchers. The surrounding street was cobbled and the sky was white with clouds. His smile looked almost reluctant, like a man used to being behind the camera not in front of it. He was holding something – a coffee cup or an ice cream, I wasn't quite sure.

The second picture was a close up of his nose, moustache and chin. It wasn't the best photo to sell yourself with, but it was funny and caught my interest. I clicked on his profile and scrolled straight to his profile ad only to find it was written in French. All those school lessons where I'd sat at the back, not paying attention came back to me. I could translate three/maybe four words. I checked the rest of his profile. He lived in Paris.

It was the first time I'd received a message from someone living abroad. I had no idea my profile could even be viewed by men overseas. I was in a playful mood, so I responded. I'd had brief conversations in the past with men in the UK who lived in the north or far west or places other than London. Quite often they were dabbling (ie they weren't seriously looking, they just fancied a chat or a flirt). Sometimes a brief, funny or interesting chat is just what you need to remind yourself that you're attractive to the opposite sex. Sometimes it's the thing that keeps you going when you're beginning to wonder exactly when you'll meet someone. Invariably those conversations would consist of a few days of playful messaging before we'd agree that the distance would never work. I imagined this would be the same.

I sent a reply back, thanking him for his message and his compliment. His name was Gérard. We exchanged a few more messages over the next few days. His messages were polite and complimentary but neither of us attempted to delve beneath the surface of each other's lives. I don't know why I continued to reply to him. He intrigued me, yes, but I knew it wouldn't go anywhere. These things never do. But Gérard continued to send messages and I replied in an equally polite manner.

Then one day his messages stopped. I assumed I'd been ghosted and deleted him from my inbox. Now I no longer had to wait or speculate about when or if he would contact me again. I could also no longer see if he was online and possibly deliberately ignoring me. In short, I put him back in the stranger realm and let him drift out of my mind.

A couple of weeks later, a new message arrived in my Inbox from Gérard. It said simply, 'Time has no hold over you.' Interesting choice of words and persistent – both qualities I liked – so I sent a reply. Soon our messages were back to where we were before he disappeared, which he explained was because of a two-week summer holiday with his daughter.

About a week later, he asked me something that would change the way we communicated going forward. In one long email he asked if I'd ever considered a long-distance relationship. It wasn't something I'd given any thought to. Mainly because I assumed the site would only introduce me to men living in the UK. I answered as honestly as I could – it wasn't something I'd planned or expected but I had an open mind about it. I remembered Sherrill who'd found her fiancé only after she'd widened her search to 100 miles. 'Who knows where you'll meet your partner?' she'd said.

After a couple of weeks, we exchanged emails. He wrote beautiful and engaging messages. Over two weeks we emailed each other almost every day – our messages growing longer and longer with each newly composed mail. I learned more about him from his messages. He also sent more pictures. He had a kind, gentle face and his pictures matched the tone of his emails.

We both enjoyed writing to each other so when he suggested exchanging telephone numbers, sending text messages through What's app followed. Everything was moving at just the right pace.

Straight talking

Our first phone conversation followed a short game of What'sApp ping pong. We were getting to know each other through our words, I'd seen him in pictures and, so far, I liked him. But hearing someone speak adds a whole new level of attraction. Voice and tone are important. They can be the things that turn you off or lead you deeper in. Sound is a significant sense in our attraction to other people. We connect to the sound of someone's voice in a unique way. Your voice can be squeaky or mellifluous or a whole range of possibilities in between. The one thing it will do is give the person you're speaking to more of an impression of you as a person.

I was nervous before that first call and he admitted via

What'sApp that he was too. I liked the ease with which he showed his vulnerability. Having been through this before I knew each new step on the dating ladder could be the one to end it all. In fact, I told myself that it would end here. It was part insecurity, part preparing for the worst. If I thought it would go badly then I'd have no expectations. It would be difficult to feel disappointed if I'd convinced myself of the worst possible scenario.

When he called all this was still going around in my head. First impressions: he sounded a little nervous too. But his voice was warm, relaxed, animated and smiley. We chatted easily. There were moments when we asked each other to repeat something but we had no problem understanding each other. When he spoke French his voice settled into it's own beautiful rhythm. If you know French you'll know there are sounds and stresses we make in English that are difficult for a native French speaker. So when Gérard spoke French it sounded right. It suited his voice, and his pitch and tone changed. In French his voice sounded comfortable, rich and sensuous.

We Skyped a few days later. By now I knew I liked him. I wanted to like how he moved. Photos are good, but even if they're an accurate representation, they only capture a person in a fraction of a second. They can't show you how a person moves, how they'll be in reality. Skype gives you that when physical proximity can't. Beforehand, I admit, I had mixed feelings. There was that part of me that really wanted to like him. To feel attracted to him. Then there was the side that was rooting for the opposite side. This would be the stage that ended it all. You won't like him said a loud, negative voice in my head. There'll be something about him that puts you off. He won't look like his picture. He'll have gone through a personality transplant since your last conversation. He'll come across all sleazy... I was, of course, dampening my own expectations. I just needed to not have too much hope. At this stage if hope is in abundance you're in trouble if disappointment rears its ugly head.

He called me.

Please let me like him, please let me like him...

I pressed connect.

Immediately I could see myself in the corner of the screen. But I couldn't see him. His video camera was off. Straightaway the neg voice kicked in. Ah, you see, he must be dodgy. His camera's off. But he apologized and a second later his face materialized on the screen in front of me. He had the same gentle look as the photo on his whats app profile and was exactly how I imagined him. He was attractive, witty, intelligent, thoughtful... Thinking back, that first conversation exhausted my bank of positive adjectives. We shared the same humour so we laughed a lot. I liked the way he carried himself, the way he moved, his thought processes, his gentlemanly nature. Our first Skype conversation lasted two hours and was followed by many more of the same. We also continued to text, email and speak on the phone. We were communicating in almost every way it was possible to. And with each form we were sharing more about each other without having the physical pressures that being in the same country would, by now, have imposed on us. It also meant we followed my own ethos fully and showed how effectively it worked to help you get to know a person.

Three months after receiving Gérard's first website message we agreed to meet for our first date. His train came in at 10am on a Saturday morning in August. I arrived at St Pancras early, waiting nervously among a mixed bag of people near the exit for Eurostar arrivals. When the train arrived people peeled away from the waiting group one by one as a loved one came through. They'd hug passionately, then kiss and head off for the train or bus to wherever their journey would continue. I waited so long I began to wonder whether I had the right train. That's when I saw him. He looked cool and relaxed in that French way. It was because of all the ways we'd been in contact up to now that meeting him felt like the most natural thing. We too hugged and kissed and went on to have the most perfect day together, exploring London like children. And at 8pm I watched him go through the departure gate at St Pancras with a kiss and a promise that this was the first of many more meetings.

BIBLIOGRAPHY

Beldo, Sarah. "Fraud in the world of online Dating". (February 14, 2018) Sift Science. https://blog.siftscience.com/2018/online-dating-fraud-infographic/

Booher, Diane. "Gender Negotiation Communication Style Differences: Women." (August 27, 2010) http://www.negotiations.com/articles/gender-bender/

Cowie, Claire. "Gender Language." July 2000. (August 29, 2010) http://www.lingutronic.de/Studium/Anglistik/Gender%20Language/Gender%20Language.pdf

eHarmony, "Over 50% of couples will meet online by 2031", https://www.eharmony.co.uk/dating-advice/online-dating-unplugged/over-50-of-couples-will-meet-online-by-2031#.WthHu9NubEY

Get Safe Online. "Love Hurts: Valentine's Fraud Warning". (February 13, 2018) https://www.getsafeonline.org/news/love-hurts-valentines-fraud-warning/

Hooson, Marie. "Happy Faces Really Are Healthy Faces". Swansea University (September, 2017) http://www.swansea.ac.uk/press-office/news-archive/2017/happyfacesreallyarehealthyfaces.php

Hughes, Susan M., Mogilski, Justin K., Harrison, Melissa A. "The Perception and Parameters of Intentional Voice Manipulation".

(Setpember 2013) Journal of Nonverbal Behaviour

McManus, Barbara F. "Gender and Modes of Communication." March 1999. (August 27, 2010) http://www2.cnr.edu/home/bmcmanus/gendercom.html

McGrath, Rebecca. "Online Dating UK - January 2015." Mintel.

Murray, Meghan. "Men Tell Us What They Want to See in a Dating Message". Zoosk survey (October 31, 2017) https://www.zoosk.com/date-mix/online-dating-advice/online-dating-first-message/dating-message-what-men-want/

Radicati. "Email Statistics Report, 2009-2013." May 6, 2009. (August 30, 2010) http://www.radicati.com/?p=3237

Rosetti, Paolo. "Gender Differences in Email Communication." The Internet TESL Journal. Vol. 4, No. 7. July 1998. (August 30, 2010) http://iteslj.org/Articles/Rossetti-GenderDif.html

Smith, Matthew. "How many dates should you wait before having sex with somone". (March 30, 2017) YouGov poll. https://yougov.co.uk/news/2017/03/30/how-many-dates-should-you-wait-having-sex-someone/

Tannen, Deborah. "Sex, Lies, and Conversation." The Washington Post. June 24, 1990. (August 27, 2010) https://www9.georgetown.edu/faculty/tannend/sexlies.htm

Tannen, Deborah. "That's Not What I Meant." Ballantine Books. 1986.

Tannen, Deborah. "The Power of Talk: Who Gets Heard and Why." Harvard Business Review. September-October 1995. (August 27, 2010) http://www9.georgetown.edu/faculty/tannend/pdfs/the_power_of_talk.pdf

Tannen, Deborah. "Who Does the Talking Here?" The Washington Post. Sunday, July 15, 2007. (August 27, 2010) http://www.washingtonpost.com/wp-dyn/content/article/2007/07/13/AR2007071301815.html

Torppa, Cynthia Burggraf. "Gender Issues: Communication Differences in Interpersonal Relationships." The Ohio State University Extension. 2010. [September 3, 2010]

Whitworth, Damian. "Why Men and Women Argue Differently." The Times. October 30, 2007. (August 27, 2010) http://www.timesonline.co.uk/tol/life_and_style/men/article2764731.ece

29800140R00112

Printed in Great
Britain
by Amazon